CH00689685

DEFENSE AGAINST THE ARIANS

- *ST. ATHANASIUS* -

Copyright © 2014 Beloved Publishing

All rights reserved. No part of this book may be reproduced, scanned, or distributed in any printed or electronic form without permission.

Printed in the United States of America

ISBN:

Table of Contents:

Chapter 1

Introduction. 1. I supposed that, after so many proofs of my innocence had been given, my enemies would have shrunk from further enquiry, and would now have condemned themselves for their false accusations of others. But as they are not yet abashed, though they have been so clearly convicted, but, as insensible to shame, persist in their slanderous reports against me, professing to think that the whole matter ought to be tried over again (not that they may have judgment passed on them, for that they avoid, but in order to harass me, and to disturb the minds of the simple); I therefore thought it necessary to make my defence unto you, that you may listen to their murmurings no longer, but may denounce their wickedness and base calumnies. And it is only to you, who are men of sincere minds, that I offer a defence: as for the contentious, I appeal confidently to the decisive proofs which I have against them. For my cause needs no further judgment; for judgment has already been given, and not once or twice only, but many times. First of all, it was tried in my own country in an assembly of nearly one hundred of its Bishops; a second time at Rome, when, in consequence of letters from Eusebius, both they and we were summoned, and more than fifty Bishops met; and a third time in the great Council assembled at Sardica by order of the most religious Emperors Constantius and Constans, when my enemies were degraded as false accusers, and the sentence that was passed in my favour received the suffrages of more than three hundred Bishops, out of the provinces of Egypt, Libya, and Pentapolis, Palestine, Arabia, Isauria, Cyprus, Pamphylia, Lycia, Galatia, Dacia, Moesia, Thrace, Dardania, Macedonia, Epirus, Thessaly, Achaia, Crete, Dalmatia, Siscia, Pannonia, Noricum, Italy, Picenum, Tuscany, Campania, Calabria, Apulia, Bruttia, Sicily, the whole of Africa, Sardinia, Spain, Gaul, and Britain.

Added to these was the testimony of Ursacius and Valens, who had formerly calumniated me, but afterwards changed their minds, and not only gave their assent to the sentence that was passed in my favour, but also confessed that they themselves and the rest of my enemies were false accusers; for men who make such a change and such a recantation of course reflect upon Eusebius and his fellows, for with them they had contrived the plot against me. Now after a matter has been examined and decided on such clear evidence by so many eminent Bishops, every one will confess that further discussion is unnecessary; else, if an investigation be instituted at this time, it may be again discussed and again investigated, and there will be no end to such trifling.

2. Now the decision of so many Bishops was sufficient to confound those who would still fain pretend some charge against me. But when my

enemies also bear testimony in my favour and against themselves, declaring that the proceedings against me were a conspiracy, who is there that would not be ashamed to doubt any longer? The law requires that in the mouth of two or three witnesses judgments shall be settled, and we have here this great multitude of witnesses in my favour, with the addition of the proofs afforded by my enemies; so much so that those who still continue opposed to me no longer attach any importance to their own arbitraryjudgment, but now have recourse to violence, and in the place of fair reasoning seek to injurethose by whom they were exposed. For this is the chief cause of vexation to them, that the measures they carried on in secret, contrived by themselves in a corner, have been brought to light and disclosed by Valens and Ursacius; for they are well aware that their recantation while it clears those whom they have injured, condemns themselves.

Indeed this led to their degradation in the Council of Sardica, as mentioned before; and with good reason; for, as the Pharisees of old, when they undertook the defence of Paul. , fully exposed the conspiracy which they and the Jews had formed against him; and as the blessed David was proved to be persecuted unjustly when the persecutor confessed, I have sinned, my son David;' so it was with these men; being overcome by the truth they made a request, and delivered it in writing to Julius, Bishop of Rome. They wrote also to me requesting to be on terms of peace with me, though they have spread such reports concerning me; and probably even now they are covered with shame, on seeing that those whom they sought to destroy by the grace of the Lord are still alive. Consistently also with this conduct they anathematized Arius and his heresy; for knowing that Eusebius and his fellows had conspired against me in behalf of their own misbelief, and of nothing else, as soon as they had determined to confess their calumnies against me, they immediately renounced also that antichristian heresy for the sake of which they had falsely asserted them.

The following are the letters written in my favour by the Bishops in the several Councils and first the letter of the Egyptian Bishops.

Encyclical Letter of the Council of Egypt. The holy Council assembled at Alexandria out of Egypt, the Thebais, Libya, and Pentapolis, to the Bishops of the Catholic Church everywhere, brethren beloved and greatly longed for in the Lord, greeting.

3. Dearly beloved brethren, we might have put forth a defence of our brother Athanasius as respects the conspiracy of Eusebius and his fellows against him, and complained of his sufferings at their hands, and have exposed all their false charges, either at the beginning of their conspiracy or upon his arrival at Alexandria. But circumstances did not permit it then, as you also know; and lately, after the return of

the Bishop Athanasius, we thought that they would be confounded and covered with shame at their manifest injustice: in consequence we prevailed with ourselves to remain silent. Since, however, after all his severe sufferings, after his retirement into Gaul, after his sojourn in a foreign and far distant country in the place of his own, after his narrow escape from death through their calumnies, but thanks to the clemency of the Emperor,—distress which would have satisfied even the most cruel enemy,—they are still insensible to shame, are again acting insolently against the Church and Athanasius; and from indignation at his deliverance venture on still more atrocious schemes against him, and are ready with an accusation, fearless of the words in holy Scripture, A false witness shall not be unpunished;' and, The mouth that belieth slayeth the soul;' we therefore are unable longer to hold our peace, being amazed at their wickedness and at the insatiable love of contention displayed in their intrigues.

For see, they cease not to disturb the ear of royalty with fresh reports against us; they cease not to write letters of deadly import, for the destruction of the Bishop who is the enemy of their impiety. For again have they written to the Emperors against him; again they wish to conspire against him, charging him with a butchery which has never taken place; again they wish to shed his blood, accusing him of a murder that never was committed (for at that former time would they have murdered him by their calumnies, had we not had a kind Emperor); again they are urgent, to say the least, that he should be sent into banishment, while they pretend to lament the miseries of those alleged to have been exiled by him. They lament before us things that have never been done, and, not satisfied with what has been done to him, desire to add thereto other and more cruel treatment. So mild are they and merciful, and of so just a disposition; or rather (for the truth shall be spoken) so wicked are they and malicious; obtaining respect through fear and by threats, rather than by their piety and justice, as becomes Bishops. They have dared in their letters to the Emperors to pour forth language such as no contentious person would employ even among those that are without; they have charged him with a number of murders and butcheries, and that not before a Governor, or any other superior officer, but before the three Augusti; nor shrink they from any journey however long, provided only all greater courts may be filled with their accusations. For indeed, dearly beloved, their business consists in accusations, and that of the most solemn character, forasmuch as the tribunals to which they make their appeal are the most solemn of any upon earth. And what other end do they propose by these investigations, except to move the Emperor to capital punishment?

4. Their own conduct therefore, and not that of Athanasius, is the fittest subject for lamentation and mourning, and one would more properly lament

them, for such actions ought to be bewailed, since it is written, Weep ye not for the dead, neither bemoan him: but weep sore for him that goeth away, for he shall return no more.' For their whole letter contemplates nothing but death; and their endeavour is to kill, whenever they may be permitted, or if not, to drive into exile. And this they were permitted to do by the most religious father of the Emperors, who gratified their fury by the banishment of Athanasius, instead of his death. Now that this is not the conduct even of ordinary Christians, scarcely even of heathens, much less of Bishops, who profess to teach others righteousness, we suppose that your Christian consciences must at once perceive. How can they forbid others to accuse their brethren, who themselves become their accusers, and that to the Emperors? How can they teach compassion for the misfortunes of others, who cannot rest satisfied even with our banishment? For there was confessedly a general sentence of banishment against us Bishops, and we all looked upon ourselves as banished men: and now again we consider ourselves as restored with Athanasius to our native places, and instead of our former lamentations and mourning over him, as having the greatest encouragement and grace,–which may the Lord continue to us, nor suffer Eusebius and his fellows to destroy?

Even if their charges against him were true, here is a certain charge against them, that against the precept of Christianity, and after his banishment and trials, they have assaulted him again, and accuse him of murder, and butchery, and other crimes, which they sound in the royal ears against the Bishops. But how manifold is their wickedness, and what manner of men think you them, when every word they speak is false, every charge they bring a calumny, and there is no truth whatever either in their mouths or their writings! Let us then at length enter upon these matters, and meet their last charges. This will prove, that in their former representations in the Council and at the trial their conduct was dishonourable, or rather their words untrue, besides exposing them for what they have now advanced.

5. We are indeed ashamed to make any defence against such charges. But since our reckless accusers lay hold of any charge, and allege that murders and butcheries were committed after the return of Athanasius, we beseech you to bear with our answer though it be somewhat long; for circumstances constrain us. No murder has been committed either by Athanasius or on his account, since our accusers, as we said before, compel us to enter upon this humiliating defence. Slaughter and imprisonment are foreign to our Church. No one did Athanasius commit into the hands of the executioner; and the prison, so far as he was concerned, was never disturbed. Our sanctuaries are now, as they have always been, pure, and honoured only with the Blood of Christ and His pious worship. Neither

Presbyter nor Deacon was destroyed by Athanasius; he perpetrated no murder, he caused the banishment of no one. Would that they had never caused the like to him, nor given him actual experience of it! No one here has been banished on his account; no one at all except Athanasius himself, the Bishop of Alexandria, whom they banished, and whom, now that he is restored, they again seek to entangle in the same or even a more cruel plot than before, setting their tongues to speak all manner of false and deadly words against him.

For, behold, they now attribute to him the acts of the magistrates; and although they plainly confess in their letter that the Prefect of Egypt passed sentence upon certain persons, they now are not ashamed to impute this sentence to Athanasius; and that, though he had not at the time entered Alexandria, but was yet on his return from his place of exile. Indeed he was then in Syria; since we must needs adduce in defence his length of way from home, that a man may not be responsible for the actions of a Governor or Prefect of Egypt. But supposing Athanasius had been in Alexandria, what were the proceedings of the Prefect to Athanasius? However, he was not even in the country; and what the Prefect of Egypt did was not done on ecclesiastical grounds, but for reasons which you will learn from the records, which, after we understood what they had written, we made diligent enquiry for, and have transmitted to you. Since then they now raise a cry against certain things which were never done either by him or for him, as though they had certainly taken place, and testify against such evils as though they were assured of their existence; let them inform us from what Council they obtained their knowledge of them, from what proofs, and from what judicial investigation? But if they have no such evidence to bring forward, and nothing but their own mere assertion, we leave it to you to consider as regards their former charges also, how the things took place, and why they so speak of them. In truth, it is nothing but calumny, and a plot of our enemies, and a temper of ungovernable mood, and an impiety in behalf of the Arian madmen which is frantic against true godliness, and desires to root out the orthodox, so that henceforth the advocates of impiety may preach without fear whatever doctrines they please. The history of the matter is as follows:–

6. When Arius, from whom the heresy of the Arian madmen has its name, was cast out of the Church for his impiety by Bishop Alexander, of blessed memory, Eusebius and his fellows, who are the disciples and partners of his impiety, considering themselves also to have been ejected, wrote frequently to Bishop Alexander, beseeching him not to leave the heretic Arius out of the Church. But when Alexander in his piety towards Christ refused to admit that impious man, they directed their resentment against Athanasius, who was then a Deacon, because in their busy enquiries they had

heard that he was much in the familiarity of Bishop Alexander, and much honoured by him. And their hatred of him was greatly increased after they had experience of his piety towards Christ, in the Council assembled at Nicaea, wherein he spoke boldly against the impiety of the Arian madmen. But when God raised him to the Episcopate, their long-cherished malice burst forth into a flame, and fearing his orthodoxy and resistance of their impiety, they (and especially Eusebius [486] , who was smitten with a consciousness of his own evil doings), engaged in all manner of treacherous designs against him. They prejudiced the Emperor against him; they frequently threatened him with Councils; and at last assembled at Tyre; and to this day they cease not to write against him, and are so implacable that they even find fault with his appointment to the Episcopate, taking every means of shewing their enmity and hatred towards him, and spreading false reports for the sole purpose of thereby vilifying his character.

However, the very misrepresentations which they now are making do but convict their former statements of being falsehoods, and a mere conspiracy against him. For they say, that after the death of Bishop Alexander, a certain few having mentioned the name of Athanasius, six or seven Bishops elected him clandestinely in a secret place:' and this is what they wrote to the Emperors, having no scruple about asserting the greatest falsehoods.

Now that the whole multitude and all the people of the Catholic Church assembled together as with one mind and body, and cried, shouted, that Athanasius should be Bishop of their Church, made this the subject of their public prayers to Christ, and conjured us to grant it for many days and nights, neither departing themselves from the Church, nor suffering us to do so; of all this we are witnesses, and so is the whole city, and the province too. Not a word did they speak against him, as these persons represented, but gave him the most excellent titles they could devise, calling him good, pious, Christian, an ascetic, a genuine Bishop. And that he was elected by a majority of our body in the sight and with the acclamations of all the people, we who elected him also testify, who are surely more credible witnesses than those who were not present, and now spread these false accounts.

But yet Eusebius finds fault with the appointment of Athanasius,–he who perhaps never received any appointment to his office at all; or if he did, has himself rendered it invalid. For he had first the See of Berytus, but leaving that he came to Nicomedia. He left the one contrary to the law, and contrary to the law invaded the other; having deserted his own without affection, and holding possession of another's without reason; he lost his love for the first in his lust for another, without even keeping to that which he obtained at the prompting of his lust. For, behold, withdrawing himself from the second, again he takes possession of another's, casting an evil eye all around him upon the cities of other men, and thinking that godliness consists in wealth and in the greatness of cities, and making light of the heritage of God to which he had been appointed; not knowing that where' even two or three are gathered in the name of the' Lord, there' is the Lord in the midst of them;' not considering the words of the Apostle, I will not boast in another man's labours;' not perceiving the charge which he has given, Art thou bound unto a wife? seek not to be loosed.' For if this expression applies to a wife, how much more does it apply to a Church, and to the same Episcopate; to which whosoever is bound ought not to seek another, lest he prove an adulterer according to holy Scripture.

7. But though conscious of these his own misdoings, he has boldly undertaken to arraign the appointment of Athanasius, to which honourable testimony has been borne by all, and he ventures to reproach him with his deposition, though he has been deposed himself, and has a standing proof of his deposition in the appointment of another in his room. How could either he or Theognius depose another, after they had been deposed themselves, which is sufficiently proved by the appointment of others in their room? For you know very well that there were appointed instead of them Amphion to Nicomedia and Chrestus to Nicaea, in consequence of their own impiety and connection with the Arian madmen,

who were rejected by the Ecumenic Council. But while they desire to set aside that true Council, they endeavour to give that name to their own unlawful combination; while they are unwilling that the decrees of the Council should be enforced, they desire to enforce their own decisions; and they use the name of a Council, while they refuse to submit themselves to one so great as this. Thus they care not for Councils, but only pretend to do so in order that they may root out the orthodox, and annul the decrees of the true and great Council against the Arians, in support of whom, both now and heretofore, they have ventured to assert these falsehoods against the Bishop Athanasius. For their former statements resembled those they now falsely make, viz., that disorderly meetings were held at his entrance, with lamentation and mourning, the people indignantly refusing to receive him. Now such was not the case, but, quite the contrary, joy and cheerfulness prevailed, and the people ran together, hastening to obtain the desired sight of him. The churches were full of rejoicings, and thanksgivings were offered up to the Lord everywhere; and all the Ministers and Clergy beheld him with such feelings, that their souls were possessed with delight, and they esteemed that the happiest day of their lives. Why need we mention the inexpressible joy that prevailed among us Bishops, for we have already said that we counted ourselves to have been partakers in his sufferings?

8. Now this being confessedly the truth of the matter, although it is very differently represented by them, what weight can be attached to that Council or trial of which they make their boast? Since they presume thus to interfere in a case which they did not witness, which they have not examined, and for which they did not meet, and to write as though they were assured of the truth of their statements, how can they claim credit respecting these matters for the consideration of which they say that they did meet together? Will it not rather be believed that they have acted both in the one case and in the other out of enmity to us? For what kind of a Council of Bishops was then held? Was it an assembly which aimed at the truth? Was not almost every one among them our enemy? Did not the attack of Eusebius and his fellows upon us proceed from their zeal for the Arian madness? Did they not urge on the others of their party? Have we not always written against them as professing the doctrines of Arius? Was not Eusebius of Caesarea in Palestine accused by our confessors of sacrificing to idols? Was not George proved to have been deposed by the blessed Alexander? Were not they charged with various offences, some with this, some with that?

How then could such men entertain the purpose of holding a meeting against us? How can they have the boldness to call that a Council, at which a Count presided, which an executioner attended, and where an usher instead of the Deacons of the Church introduced us into Court; and where the Count only spoke, and all present held their peace, or rather obeyed his directions? The removal of those Bishops who seemed to deserve it was prevented at his desire; and when he gave the order we were dragged about by soldiers;–or rather Eusebius and his fellows gave the order, and he was subservient to their will. In short, dearly beloved, what kind of Council was that, the object of which was banishment and murder at the pleasure of the Emperor? And of what nature were their charges?–for here is matter of still greater astonishment. There was one Arsenius whom they declared to have been murdered; and they also complained that a chalice belonging to the sacred mysteries had been broken.

Now Arsenius is alive, and prays to be admitted to our communion. He waits for no other testimony to prove that he is still living, but himself confesses it, writing in his own person to our brother Athanasius, whom they positively asserted to be his murderer. The impious wretches were not ashamed to accuse him of having murdered a man who was at a great distance from him, being separated by so great a distance, whether by sea or land, and whose abode at that time no one knew. Nay, they even had the boldness to remove him out of sight, and place him in concealment, though he had suffered no injury; and, if it had been possible, they would have transported him to another world, nay, or have taken him from life in earnest, so that either by a true or false statement of his murder they might in good earnest destroy Athanasius. But thanks to divine Providence for this also which permitted them not to succeed in their injustice, but presented Arsenius alive to the eyes of all men, who has clearly proved their conspiracy and calumnies. He does not withdraw from us as murderers, nor hate us as having injured him (for indeed he has suffered no evil at all); but he desires to hold communion with us; he wishes to be numbered among us, and has written to this effect.

9. Nevertheless they laid their plot against Athanasius, accusing him of having murdered a person who was still alive; and those same men are the authors of his banishment. For it was not the father of the Emperors, but their calumnies, that sent him into exile. Consider whether this is not the truth. When nothing was discovered to the prejudice of our fellow-minister Athanasius, but still the Count threatened him with violence, and was very zealous against him, the Bishop fled from this violence and went up to the most religious Emperor, where he protested against the Count and their conspiracy against him, and requested either that a lawful Council of Bishops might be assembled, or that the Emperor would himself receive his defence concerning the charges they brought against him. Upon this the Emperor wrote in anger, summoning them before him, and declaring that he would hear the cause himself, and for that purpose he also

ordered a Council to be held. Whereupon Eusebius and his fellows went up and falsely charged Athanasius, not with the same offences which they had published against him at Tyre, but with an intention of detaining the vessels laden with corn, as though Athanasius had been the man to pretend that he could stop the exports of corn from Alexandria to Constantinople.

Certain of our friends were present at the palace with Athanasius, and heard the threats of the Emperor upon receiving this report. And when Athanasius cried out upon the calumny, and positively declared that it was not true, (for how, he argued, should he a poor man, and in a private station, be able to do such a thing?) Eusebius did not hesitate publicly to repeat the charge, and swore that Athanasius was a rich man, and powerful, and able to do anything; in order that it might thence be supposed that he had used this language. Such was the accusation these venerable Bishops proffered against him. But the grace of God proved superior to their wickedness, for it moved the pious Emperor to mercy, who instead of death passed upon him the sentence of banishment. Thus their calumnies, and nothing else, were the cause of this. For the Emperor, in the letter which he previously wrote, complained of their conspiracy, censured their machinations, and condemned the Meletians as unscrupulous and deserving of execration; in short, expressed himself in the severest terms concerning them. For he was greatly moved when he heard the story of the dead alive; he was moved at hearing of murder in the case of one alive, and not deprived of life. We have sent you the letter.

10. But these marvellous men, Eusebius and his fellows, to make a show of refuting the truth of the case, and the statements contained in this letter, put forward the name of a Council, and ground its proceedings upon the authority of the Emperor. Hence the attendance of a Count at their meeting, and the soldiers as guards of the Bishops, and royal letters compelling the attendance of any persons whom they required. But observe here the strange character of their machinations, and the inconsistency of their bold measures, so that by some means or other they may take Athanasius away from us. For if as Bishops they claimed for themselves alone the judgment of the case, what need was there for the attendance of a Count and soldiers? or how was it that they assembled under the sanction of royal letters? Or if they required the Emperor's countenance and wished to derive their authority from him, why were they then annulling his judgment? and when he declared in the letter which he wrote, that the Meletians were calumniators, unscrupulous, and that Athanasius was most innocent, and made much stir about the pretended murder of the living, how was it that they determined that the Meletians had spoken the truth, and that Athanasius was guilty of the offence; and

were not ashamed to make the living dead, living both after the Emperor's judgment, and at the time when they met together, and who even until this day is amongst us? So much concerning the case of Arsenius.

11. And as for the cup belonging to the mysteries, what was it, or where was it broken by Macarius? for this is the report which they spread up and down. But as for Athanasius, even his accusers would not have ventured to blame him, had they not been suborned by them. However, they attribute the origin of the offence to him; although it ought not to be imputed even to Macarius who is clear of it. And they are not ashamed to parade the sacred mysteries before Catechumens, and worse than that, even before heathens: whereas, they ought to attend to what is written, It is good to keep close the secret of a king;' and as the Lord has charged us, Give not that which is holy unto the dogs, neither cast ye your pearls before swine.' We ought not then to parade the holy mysteries before the uninitiated, lest the heathen in their ignorance deride them, and the Catechumens being over-curious be offended. However, what was the cup, and where and before whom was it broken? It is the Meletians who make the accusation, who are not worthy of the least credit, for they have been schismatics and enemies of the Church, not of a recent date, but from the times of the blessed Peter, Bishop and Martyr. They formed a conspiracy against Peter himself; they

calumniated his successor Achillas; they accused Alexander even before the Emperor; and being thus well versed in these arts, they have now transferred their enmity to Athanasius, acting altogether in accordance with their former wickedness. For as they slandered those that have been before him, so now they have slandered him. But their calumnies and false accusations have never prevailed against him until now, that they have got Eusebius and his fellows for their assistants and patrons, on account of the impiety which these have adopted from the Arian madmen, which has led them to conspire against many Bishops, and among the rest Athanasius.

Now the place where they say the cup was broken, was not a Church; there was no Presbyter in occupation of the place; and the day on which they say that Macarius did the deed, was not the Lord's day. Since then there was no church there; since there was no one to perform the sacred office; and since the day did not require the use of it; what was this cup belonging to the mysteries, and when, or where was it broken? There are many cups, it is plain, both in private houses, and in the public market; and if a person breaks one of them, he is not guilty of impiety. But the cup which belongs to the mysteries, and which if it be broken intentionally, makes the perpetrator of the deed an impious person, is found only among those who lawfully preside. This is the only description that can be given of this kind of cup; there is none other; this you legally give to the people to drink; this you have received according to the canon of the Church; this belongs only to those who preside over the Catholic Church, for to you only it appertains to administer the Blood of Christ, and to none besides. But as he who breaks the cup belonging to the mysteries is an impious person, much more impious is he who treats the Blood of Christ with contumely: and he does so who does this' contrary to the rule of the Church. (We say this, not as if a cup even of the schismatics was broken by Macarius, for there was no cup there at all; how should there be? where there was neither Lord's house nor any the belonging to the Church, nay, it was not the time of the celebration of the mysteries). Now such a person is the notorious Ischyras, who was never appointed to his office by the Church, and when Alexander admitted the Presbyters that had been ordained by Meletius, he was not even numbered amongst them; and therefore did not receive ordination even from that quarter.

12. By what means then did Ischyras become a Presbyter? who was it that ordained him? was it Colluthus? for this is the only supposition that remains. But it is well known and no one has any doubt about the matter that Colluthus died a Presbyter, and that every ordination of his was invalid, and that all that were ordained by him during the schism were reduced to the condition of laymen, and in that rank appear in the congregation.

How then can it be believed that a private person, occupying a private house had in his possession a sacred chalice? But the truth is, they gave the name of Presbyter at the time to a private person, and gratified him with this title to support him in his iniquitous conduct towards us; and now as the reward of his accusations they procure for him the erection of a Church. So that this man had then no Church; but as the reward of his malice and subserviency to them in accusing us, he receives now what he had not before; nay, perhaps they have even remunerated his services with the Episcopate, for so he goes about reporting, and accordingly behaves towards us with great insolence. Thus are such rewards as these now bestowed by Bishops upon accusers and calumniators though indeed it is reasonable, in the case of an accomplice, that as they have made him a partner in their proceedings, so they should also make him their associate in their own Episcopate. But this is not all; give ear yet further to their proceedings at that time.

13. Being unable to prevail against the truth, though they had thus set themselves in array against it, and Ischyras having proved nothing at Tyre, but being shewn to be a calumniator, and the calumny ruining their plot, they defer proceedings for fresh evidence, and profess that they are going to send to the Mareotis certain of their party to enquire diligently into the matter. Accordingly they dispatched secretly, with the assistance of the civil power,

persons to whom we openly objected on many accounts, as being of the party of Arius, and therefore our enemies; namely, Diognius, Maris, Theodorus, Macedonius, and two others, young both in years and mind, Ursacius and Valens from Pannonia; who, after they had undertaken this long journey for the purpose of sitting in judgment upon their enemy, set out again from Tyre for Alexandria. They did not shrink from becoming witnesses themselves, although they were the judges, but openly adopted every means of furthering their design, and undertook any labour or journey whatsoever in order to bring to a successful issue the conspiracy which was in progress. They left the Bishop Athanasius detained in a foreign country while they themselves entered their enemy's city, as if to have their revel both against his Church and against his people. And what was more outrageous still, they took with them the accuser Ischyras, but would not permit Macarius, the accused person, to accompany them, but left him in custody at Tyre. For Macarius the Presbyter of Alexandria' was made answerable for the charge far and near.

14. They therefore entered Alexandria alone with the accuser, their partner in lodging, board, and cup; and taking with them Philagrius the Prefect of Egypt they proceeded to the Mareotis, and there carried on the so-called investigation by themselves, all their own way, with the forementioned person. Although the Presbyters frequently begged that they might be

24

present, they would not permit them. The Presbyters both of the city and of the whole country desired to attend, that they might detect who and whence the persons were who were suborned by Ischyras. But they forbade the Ministers to be present, while they carried on the examination concerning church, cup, table, and the holy things, before the heathen; nay, worse than that, they summoned heathen witnesses during the enquiry concerning a cup belonging to the mysteries; and those persons who they affirmed were taken out of the way by Athanasius by summons of the Receiver-general, and they knew not where in the world they were, these same individuals they brought forward before themselves and the Prefect only, and avowedly used their testimony, whom they affirmed without shame to have been secreted by the Bishop Athanasius.

But here too their only object is to effect his death, and so they again pretend that persons are dead who are still alive, following the same method they adopted in the case of Arsenius. For the men are living, and are to be seen in their own country; but to you who are at a great distance from the spot they make a great stir about the matter as though they had disappeared, in order that, as the evidence is so far removed from you, they may falsely accuse our brother-minister, as though he used violence and the civil power; whereas they themselves have in all respects acted by means of that power and the countenance of others. For their proceedings in the

Mareotis were parallel to those at Tyre; and as there a Count attended with military assistance, and would permit nothing either to be said or done contrary to their pleasure, so here also the Prefect of Egypt was present with a band of men, frightening all the members of the Church, and permitting no one to give true testimony. And what was the strangest thing of all, the persons who came, whether as judges or witnesses, or, what was more likely, in order to serve their own purposes and those of Eusebius, lived in the same place with the accuser, even in his house, and there seemed to carry on the investigation as they pleased.

15. We suppose you are not ignorant what outrages they committed at Alexandria; for they are reported everywhere. Naked swords were at work against the holy virgins and brethren; scourges were at work against their persons, esteemed honourable in the sight of God, so that their feet were lamed by the stripes, whose souls are whole and sound in purity and all good works. The trades were excited against them; and the heathen multitude was set to strip them naked, to beat them, wantonly to insult them, and to threaten them with their altars and sacrifices. And one coarse fellow, as though license had now been given them by the Prefect in order to gratify the Bishops, took hold of a virgin by the hand, and dragged her towards an altar that happened to be near, imitating the practice of compelling to offer sacrifice in time of persecution. When this was done,

the virgins took to flight, and a shout of laughter was raised by the heathen against the Church; the Bishops being in the place, and occupying the very house where this was going on; and from which, in order to obtain favour with them, the virgins were assaulted with naked swords, and were exposed to all kinds of danger, and insult, and wanton violence. And this treatment they received on a fast-day, and at the hands of persons who themselves were feasting with the Bishops indoors.

16. Foreseeing these things, and reflecting that the entrance of enemies into a place is no ordinary calamity, we protested against this commission. And Alexander, Bishop of Thessalonica, considering the same, wrote to the people residing there, discovering the conspiracy, and testifying of the plot. They indeed reckon him to be one of themselves, and account him a partner in their designs; but they only prove thereby the violence they have exercised towards him. For even the profligate Ischyras himself was only induced by fear and violence to proceed in the matter, and was obliged by force to undertake the accusation. As a proof of this, he wrote himself to our brother Athanasius, confessing that nothing of the kind that was alleged had taken place there, but that he was suborned to make a false statement. This declaration he made, though he was never admitted by Athanasius as a Presbyter, nor received such a title of grace from him, nor was entrusted by way of recompense with the erection of a Church, nor

expected the bribe of a Bishopric; all of which he obtained from them in return for undertaking the accusation. Moreover, his whole family held communion with us, which they would not have done had they been injured in the slightest degree.

17. Now to prove that these things are facts and not mere assertions, we have the testimony of all the Presbyters of the Mareotis, who always accompany the Bishop in his visitations, and who also wrote at the time against Ischyras. But neither those of them who came to Tyre were allowed to declare the truth, nor could those who remained in the Mareotis obtain permission to refute the calumnies of Ischyras. The copies also of the letters of Alexander, and of the Presbyters, and of Ischyras will prove the same thing. We have sent also the letter of the father of the Emperors, in which he expresses his indignation that the murder of Arsenius was charged upon any one while the man was still alive; as also his astonishment at the variable and inconsistent character of their accusations with respect to the cup; since at one time they accused the Presbyter Macarius, at another the Bishop Athanasius, of having broken it with his hands. He declares also on the one hand that the Meletians are calumniators, and on the other that Athanasius is perfectly innocent.

And are not the Meletians calumniators, and above all John, who after coming into the Church, and communicating with us, after condemning himself, and no longer taking any part in the proceedings respecting the cup, when he saw Eusebius and his fellows zealously supporting the Arian madmen, though they had not the daring to co-operate with them openly, but were attempting to employ others as their masks, undertook a character, as an actor in the heathen theatres? The subject of the drama was a contest of Arians; the real design of the piece being their success, but John and his partizans being put on the stage and playing the parts, in order that under colour of these, the supporters of the Arians in the garb of judges might drive away the enemies of their impiety, firmly establish their impious doctrines, and bring the Arians into the Church. And those who wish to drive out true religion strive all they can to prevail by irreligion; they who have chosen the part of that impiety which wars against Christ, endeavour to destroy the enemies thereof, as though they were impious persons; and they impute to us the breaking of the cup, for the purpose of making it appear that Athanasius, equally with themselves, is guilty of impiety towards Christ.

For what means this mention of a cup belonging to the mysteries by them? Whence comes this religious regard for the cup among those who support impiety towards Christ? Whence comes it that Christ's cup is known to them who know not Christ? How can they who profess to honour that cup, dishonour the God of the cup? or how can they who lament over the cup, seek to murder the Bishop who celebrates the mysteries therewith? for they would have murdered him, had it been in their power. And how can they who lament the loss of the throne that was Episcopally covered, seek to destroy the Bishop that sat upon it, to the end that both the throne may be without its Bishop, and that the people may be deprived of godly doctrine? It was not then the cup, nor the murder, nor any of those portentous deeds they talk about, that induced them to act thus; but the forementioned heresy of the Arians, for the sake of which they conspired against Athanasius and other Bishops, and still continue to wage war against the Church. Who are they that have really been the cause of murders and banishments? Is it not these?

Who are they that, availing themselves of external support, conspire against the Bishops? Are not Eusebius and his fellows the men, and not Athanasius, as they say in their letters? Both he and others have suffered at their hands. Even at the time of which we speak, four Presbyters of Alexandria, though they had not even proceeded to Tyre, were banished by their means. Who then are they whose conduct calls for tears and lamentations? Is it not they, who after they have been guilty of one course of persecution, do not scruple to add to it a second, but have recourse to all manner of falsehood, in order that they may destroy a Bishop who will not give way to their impious heresy? Hence arises the enmity of Eusebius and his fellows; hence their proceedings at Tyre; hence their pretended trials; hence also now the letters which they have written even without any trial, expressing the utmost confidence in their statements; hence their calumnies before the father of the Emperors, and before the most religious Emperors themselves.

18. For it is necessary that you should know what is now reported to the prejudice of our fellow-minister Athanasius, in order that you may thereby be led to condemn their wickedness, and may perceive that they desire nothing else but to murder him. A quantity of corn was given by the father of the Emperors for the support of certain widows, partly of Libya, and partly certain out of Egypt. They have all received it up to this time, Athanasius getting nothing therefrom, but the trouble of assisting them. But now, although the recipients themselves make no complaint, but acknowledge that they have received it, Athanasius has been accused of selling all the corn, and appropriating the profits to his own use: and the Emperor wrote to this effect about it, charging him with the offence in consequence of the calumnies which had been raised against him. Now who are they which have raised these calumnies? Is it not those who after they have been guilty of one course of persecution, scruple not to set on foot another? Who are the authors of those letters which are said to have come from the Emperor? Are not the Arians, who are so zealous against Athanasius, and scruple not to speak and write anything against him?

No one would pass over persons who have acted as they have done, in order to entertain suspicion of others. Nay, the proof of their calumny appears to be most evident for they are anxious under cover of it, to take away the corn from the Church, and to give it to the Arians. And this circumstance more than any other, brings the matter home to the authors of this design and their principals, who scrupled neither to set on foot a charge of murder against Athanasius, as a base means of prejudicing the Emperor against him, nor yet to take away from the Clergy of the Church the subsistence of the poor, in order that in fact they might make gain for the heretics.

19. We have sent also the testimony of our fellow-ministers in Libya, Pentapolis, and Egypt, from which likewise you may learn the false accusations which have been brought against Athanasius. And these things they do, in order that, the professors of true godliness being henceforth induced by fear to remain quiet, the heresy of the impious Arians may be brought in in its stead. But thanks be to your piety, dearly beloved, that you have frequently anathematized the Arians in your letters, and have never given them admittance into the Church. The exposure of Eusebius and his fellows is also easy and ready at hand. For behold, after their former letters concerning the Arians, of which also we have sent you copies, they now openly stir up the Arian madmen against the Church, though the whole Catholic Church has anathematized them; they have

appointed a Bishop over them; they distract the Churches with threats and alarms, that they may gain assistants in their impiety in every part. Moreover, they send Deacons to the Arian madmen, who openly join their assemblies; they write letters to them, and receive answers from them, thus making schisms in the Church, and holding communion with them; and they send to every part, commending their heresy, and repudiating the Church, as you will perceive from the letters they have addressed to the Bishop of Rome and perhaps to yourselves also. You perceive therefore, dearly beloved, that these things are not undeserving of vengeance: they are indeed dreadful and alien from the doctrine of Christ.

Wherefore we have assembled together, and have written to you, to request of your Christian wisdom to receive this our declaration and sympathize with our brother Athanasius, and to shew your indignation against Eusebius and his fellows who have essayed such things, in order that such malice and wickedness may no longer prevail against the Church. We call upon you to be the avengers of such injustice, reminding you of the injunction of the Apostle, Put away from among yourselves that wicked person.' Wicked indeed is their conduct, and unworthy of your communion. Wherefore give no further heed to them, though they should again write to you against the Bishop Athanasius (for all that proceeds from them is false); not even though they subscribe their letter with names of Egyptian

Bishops. For it is evident that it will not be we who write, but the Meletians, who have ever been schismatics, and who even unto this day make disturbances and raise factions in the Churches. For they ordain improper persons, and all but heathens; and they are guilty of such actions as we are ashamed to set down in writing, but which you may learn from those whom we have sent unto you, who will also deliver to you our letter.

20. Thus wrote the Bishops of Egypt to all Bishops, and to Julius, Bishop of Rome.

Chapter 2

Letter of Julius to the Eusebians at Antioch. Eusebius and his fellows wrote also to Julius, and thinking to frighten me, requested him to call a council, and to be himself the judge, if he so pleased. When therefore I went up to Rome, Julius wrote to Eusebius and his fellows as was suitable, and sent moreover two of his own Presbyters, Elpidius and Philoxenus. But they, when they heard of me, were thrown into confusion, as not expecting my going up thither; and they declined the proposed Council, alleging unsatisfactory reasons for so doing, but in truth they were afraid lest the things should be proved against them which Valens and Ursacius afterwards confessed. However, more than fifty Bishops assembled, in the place where the Presbyter Vito held his congregation; and they acknowledged my defence, and gave me the confirmation both of their communion and their love. On the other hand, they expressed great indignation against Eusebius and his fellows, and requested that Julius would write to the following effect to those of their number who had written to him. Which accordingly he did, and sent it by the hand of Count Gabianus.

The Letter of Julius.

Julius to his dearly beloved brethren, Danius, Flacillus, Narcissus, Eusebius, Maris, Macedonius,

Theodorus, and their friends, who have written to me from Antioch, sends health in the Lord.

21. I have read your letter which was brought to me by my Presbyters Elpidius and Philoxenus, and I am surprised to find that, whereas I wrote to you in charity and with conscious sincerity, you have replied to me in an unbecoming and contentious temper; for the pride and arrogance of the writers is plainly exhibited in that letter. Yet such feelings are inconsistent with the Christian faith; for what was written in a charitable spirit ought likewise to be answered in a spirit of charity and not of contention. And was it not a token of charity to send Presbyters to sympathize with them that are in suffering, and to desire those who had written to me to come thither, that the questions at issue might obtain a speedy settlement, and all things be duly ordered, so that our brethren might no longer be exposed to suffering, and that you might escape further calumny? But something seems to shew that your temper is such, as to force us to conclude that even in the terms in which you appeared to pay honour to us, you have expressed yourselves under the disguise of irony. The Presbyters also whom we sent to you, and who ought to have returned rejoicing, did on the contrary return sorrowful on account of the proceedings they had witnessed among you. And I, when I had read your letter, after much consideration, kept it to myself, thinking that after all some of you would come, and there would be no

need to bring it forward, lest if it should be openly exhibited, it should grieve many of our brethren here. But when no one arrived, and it became necessary that the letter should be produced, I declare to you, they were all astonished, and were hardly able to believe that such a letter had been written by you at all; for it is expressed in terms of contention rather than of charity.

Now if the author of it wrote with an ambition of exhibiting his power of language, such a practice surely is more suitable for other subjects: in ecclesiastical matters, it is not a display of eloquence that is needed, but the observance of Apostolic Canons, and an earnest care not to offend one of the little ones of the Church. For it were better for a man, according to the word of the Church, that a millstone were hanged about his neck, and that he were drowned in the sea, than that he should offend even one of the little ones. But if such a letter was written, because certain persons have been aggrieved on account of their meanness of spirit towards one another (for I will not impute it to all); it were better not to entertain any such feeling of offence at all, at least not to let the sun go down upon their vexation; and certainly not to give it room to exhibit itself in writing.

22. Yet what has been done that is a just cause of vexation? or in what respect was my letter to you such? Was it, that I invited you to be present at a

council? You ought rather to have received the proposal with joy. Those who have confidence in their proceedings, or as they choose to term them, in their decisions, are not wont to be angry, if such decision is inquired into by others; they rather shew all boldness, seeing that if they have given a just decision, it can never prove to be the reverse. The Bishops who assembled in the great Council of Nicaea agreed, not without the will of God, that the decisions of one council should be examined in another, to the end that the judges, having before their eyes that other trial which was to follow, might be led to investigate matters with the utmost caution, and that the parties concerned in their sentence might have assurance that the judgment they received was just, and not dictated by the enmity of their former judges. Now if you are unwilling that such a practice should be adopted in your own case, though it is of ancient standing, and has been noticed and recommended by the great Council, your refusal is not becoming; for it is unreasonable that a custom which had once obtained in the Church, and been established by councils, should be set aside by a few individuals.

For a further reason they cannot justly take offence in this point. When the persons whom you, Eusebius and his fellows, dispatched with your letters, I mean Macarius the Presbyter, and Martyrius and Hesychius the Deacons, arrived here, and found that they were unable to withstand the arguments of the

Presbyters who came from Athanasius, but were confuted and exposed on all sides, they then requested me to call a Council together, and to write to Alexandria to the Bishop Athanasius, and also to Eusebius and his fellows, in order that a just judgment might be given in presence of all parties. And they undertook in that case to prove all the charges which had been brought against Athanasius. For Martyrius and Hesychius had been publicly refuted by us, and the Presbyters of the Bishop Athanasius had withstood them with great confidence: indeed, if one must tell the truth, Martyrius and his fellows had been utterly overthrown; and this it was that led them to desire that a Council might be held. Now supposing that they had not desired a Council, but that I had been the person to propose it, in discouragement of those who had written to me, and for the sake of our brethren who complain that they have suffered injustice; even in that case the proposal would have been reasonable and just, for it is agreeable to ecclesiastical practice, and well pleasing to God. But when those persons, whom you, Eusebius and his fellows, considered to be trustworthy, when even they wished me to call the brethren together, it was inconsistent in the parties invited to take offence, when they ought rather to have shewn all readiness to be present. These considerations shew that the display of anger in the offended persons is petulant, and the refusal of those who decline to meet the Council is unbecoming, and has a suspicious appearance. Does any one find fault, if he sees that done by another, which he would allow if done by himself? If, as you write, each council has an irreversible force, and he who has given judgment on a matter is dishonoured, if his sentence is examined by others; consider, dearly beloved, who are they that dishonour councils? who are setting aside the decisions of former judges? Not to inquire at present into every individual case, lest I should appear to press too heavily on certain parties, the last instance that has occurred, and which every one who hears it must shudder at, will be sufficient in proof of the others which I omit.

23. The Arians who were excommunicated for their impiety by Alexander, the late Bishop of Alexandria, of blessed memory, were not only proscribed by the brethren in the several cities, but were also anathematised by the whole body assembled together in the great Council of Nicaea. For theirs was no ordinary offence, neither had they sinned against man, but against our Lord Jesus Christ Himself, the Son of the living God. And yet these persons who were proscribed by the whole world, and branded in every Church, are said now to have been admitted to communion again; which I think even you ought to hear with indignation. Who then are the parties who dishonour a council? Are not they who have set at nought the votes of the Three hundred, and have preferred impiety to godliness? The heresy of the Arian madmen was condemned and proscribed by

the whole body of Bishops everywhere; but the Bishops Athanasius and Marcellus have many supporters who speak and write in their behalf. We have received testimony in favour of Marcellus, that he resisted the advocates of the Arian doctrines in the Council of Nicaea; and in favour of Athanasius, that at Tyre nothing was brought home to him, and that in the Mareotis, where the Reports against him are said to have been drawn up, he was not present. Now you know, dearly beloved, that ex parte proceedings are of no weight, but bear a suspicious appearance. Nevertheless, these things being so, we, in order to be accurate, and neither shewing any prepossession in favour of yourselves, nor of those who wrote in behalf of the other party, invited those who had written to us to come hither; that, since there were many who wrote in their behalf, all things might be enquired into in a council, and neither the guiltless might be condemned, nor the person on his trial be accounted innocent. We then are not the parties who dishonour a council, but they who at once and recklessly have received the Arians whom all had condemned, and contrary to the decision of the judges. The greater part of those judges have now departed, and are with Christ; but some of them are still in this life of trial, and are indignant at learning that certain persons have set aside their judgment.

24. We have also been informed of the following circumstance by those who were at Alexandria. A certain Carpones, who had been excommunicated by

Alexander for Arianism, was sent hither by one Gregory with certain others, also excommunicated for the same heresy. However, I had learnt the matter also from the Presbyter Macarius, and the Deacons Martyrius and Hesychius. For before the Presbyters of Athanasius arrived they urged me to send letters to one Pistus at Alexandria, though at the same time the Bishop Athanasius was there. And when the Presbyters of the Bishop Athanasius came, they informed me that this Pistus was an Arian, and that he had been excommunicated by the Bishop Alexander and the Council of Nicaea, and then ordained by one Secundus, whom also the great Council excommunicated as an Arian. This statement Martyrius and his fellows did not gainsay, nor did they deny that Pistus had received his ordination from Secundus. Now consider, after this who are most justly liable to blame? I, who could not be prevailed upon to write to the Arian Pistus; or those, who advised me to do dishonour to the great Council, and to address the irreligious as if they were religious persons? Moreover, when the Presbyter Macarius, who had been sent hither by Eusebius with Martyrius and the rest, heard of the opposition which had been made by the Presbyters of Athanasius, while we were expecting his appearance with Martyrius and Hesychius, he departed in the night, in spite of a bodily ailment; which leads us to conjecture that his departure arose from shame on account of the exposure which had been made concerning Pistus. For it is impossible that the ordination of the Arian Secundus should be considered valid in the Catholic Church. This would indeed be dishonour to the Council, and to the Bishops who composed it, if the decrees they framed, as in the presence of God, with such extreme earnestness and care, should be set aside as worthless.

25. If, as you write, the decrees of all Councils ought to be of force, according to the precedent in the case of Novatus and Paul of Samosata, all the more ought not the sentence of the Three hundred to be reversed, certainly a general Council ought not to be set at nought by a few individuals. For the Arians are heretics as they, and the like sentence has been passed both against one and the other. And, after such bold proceedings as these, who are they that have lighted up the flame of discord? for in your letter you blame us for having done this. Is it we, who have sympathised with the sufferings of the brethren, and have acted in all respects according to the Canon; or they who contentiously and contrary to the Canon have set aside the sentence of the Three hundred, and dishonoured the Council in every way? For not only have the Arians been received into communion, but Bishops also have made a practice of removing from one place to another. Now if you really believe that all Bishops have the same and equal authority, and you do not, as you assert, account of them according to the magnitude of their cities; he that is entrusted with a small city ought to abide in the place committed to

him, and not from disdain of his trust to remove to one that has never been put under him; despising that which God has given him, and making much of the vain applause of men. You ought then, dearly beloved, to have come and not declined, that the matter may be brought to a conclusion; for this is what reason demands.

But perhaps you were prevented by the time fixed upon for the Council, for you complain in your letter that the interval before the day we appointed was too short. But this, beloved, is a mere excuse. Had the day forestalled any when on the journey, the interval allowed would then have been proved to be too short. But when persons do not wish to come, and detain even my Presbyters up to the month of January, it is the mere excuse of those who have no confidence in their cause; otherwise, as I said before, they would have come, not regarding the length of the journey, not considering the shortness of the time, but trusting to the justice and reasonableness of their cause. But perhaps they did not come on account of the aspect of the times, for again you declare in your letter, that we ought to have considered the present circumstances of the East, and not to have urged you to come. Now if as you say you did not come because the times were such, you ought to have considered such times beforehand, and not to have become the authors of schism, and of mourning and lamentation in the Churches. But as the matter stands, men, who have been the cause of these things, shew that it is not the times that are to blame, but the determination of those who will not meet a Council.

26. But I wonder also how you could ever have written that part of your letter, in which you say, that I alone wrote, and not to all of you, but to Eusebius and his fellows only. In this complaint one may discover more of readiness to find fault than of regard for truth. I received the letters against Athanasius from none other than Martyrius, Hesychius and their fellows, and I necessarily wrote to them who had written against him. Either then Eusebius and his fellows ought not alone to have written, apart from you all, or else you, to whom I did not write, ought not to be offended that I wrote to them who had written to me. If it was right that I should address my letter to you all, you also ought to have written with them: but now considering what was reasonable, I wrote to them, who had addressed themselves to me, and had given me information. But if you were displeased because I alone wrote to them, it is but consistent that you should also be angry, because they wrote to me alone. But for this also, beloved, there was a fair and not unreasonable cause. Nevertheless it is necessary that I should acquaint you that, although I wrote, yet the sentiments I expressed were not those of myself alone, but of all the Bishops throughout Italy and in these parts. I indeed was unwilling to cause them all to write, lest the others should be overpowered by

their number. The Bishops however assembled on the appointed day, and agreed in these opinions, which I again write to signify to you; so that, dearly beloved, although I alone address you, yet you may be assured that these are the sentiments of all. Thus much for the excuses, not reasonable, but unjust and suspicious, which some of you have alleged for your conduct.

27. Now although what has already been said were sufficient to shew that we have not admitted to our communion our brothers Athanasius and Marcellus either too readily, or unjustly, yet it is but fair briefly to set the matter before you. Eusebius and his fellows wrote formerly against Athanasius and his fellows, as you also have written now; but a great number of Bishops out of Egypt and other provinces wrote in his favour. Now in the first place, your letters against him are inconsistent with one another, and the second have no sort of agreement with the first, but in many instances the former are answered by the latter, and the latter are impeached by the former. Now where there is this contradiction in letters, no credit whatever is due to the statements they contain. In the next place if you require us to believe what you have written, it is but consistent that we should not refuse credit to those who have written in his favour; especially, considering that you write from a distance, while they are on the spot, are acquainted with the man, and the events which are occurring there, and testify in writing to his manner of life, and

positively affirm that he has been the victim of a conspiracy throughout.

Again, a certain Bishop Arsenius was said at one time to have been made away with by Athanasius, but we have learned that he is alive, nay, that he is on terms of friendship with him. He has positively asserted that the Reports drawn up in the Mareotis were ex parte ones; for that neither the Presbyter Macarius, the accused party, was present, nor yet his Bishop, Athanasius himself. This we have learnt, not only from his own mouth, but also from the Reports which Martyrius, Hesychius and their fellows, brought to us; for we found on reading them, that the accuser Ischyras was present there, but neither Macarius, nor the Bishop Athanasius; and that the Presbyters of Athanasius desired to attend, but were not permitted. Now, beloved, if the trial was to be conducted honestly, not only the accuser, but the accused also ought to   have been present. As the accused party Macarius attended at Tyre, as well as the accuser Ischyras, when nothing was proved, so not only ought the accuser to have gone to the Mareotis, but also the accused, so that in person he might either be convicted, or by not being convicted might shew the falseness of the accusation. But now, as this was not the case, but the accuser only went out thither, with those to whom Athanasius objected, the proceedings wear a suspicious appearance.

28. And he complained also that the persons who went to the Mareotis went against his wish, for that Theognius, Maris, Theodorus, Ursacius, Valens, and Macedonius, who were the persons they sent out, were of suspected character. This he shewed not by his own assertions merely, but from the letter of Alexander who was Bishop of Thessalonica; for he produced a letter written by him to Dionysius, the Count who presided in the Council, in which he shews most clearly that there was a conspiracy on foot against Athanasius. He has also brought forward a genuine document, all in the handwriting of the accuser Ischyras himself, in which he calls God Almighty to witness that no cup was broken, nor table overthrown, but that he had been suborned by certain persons to invent these accusations. Moreover, when the Presbyters of the Mareotis arrived, they positively affirmed that Ischyras was not a Presbyter of the Catholic Church and that Macarius had not committed any such offence as the other had laid to his charge. The Presbyters and Deacons also who came to us testified in the fullest manner in favour of the Bishop Athanasius, strenuously asserting that none of those things which were alleged against him were true, but that he was the victim of a conspiracy.

And all the Bishops of Egypt and Libya wrote and protested that his ordination was lawful and strictly ecclesiastical, and that all that you had advanced against him was false, for that no murder had been committed, nor any persons despatched on his account, nor any cup broken, but that all was false. Nay, the Bishop Athanasius also shewed from the ex parte reports drawn up in the Mareotis, that a catechumen was examined and said, that he was within with Ischyras, at the time when they say Macarius the Presbyter of Athanasius burst into the place; and that others who were examined said,–one, that Ischyras was in a small cell,–and another, that he was lying down behind the door, being sick at that very time, when they say Macarius came thither. Now from these representations of his, we are naturally led to ask the question, How was it possible that a man who was lying behind the door sick could get up, conduct the service, and offer? and how could it be that Oblations were offered when catechumens were within? for if there were catechumens present, it was not yet the time for presenting the Oblations. These representations, as I said, were made by the Bishop Athanasius, and he showed from the reports, what was also positively affirmed by those who were with him, that Ischyras has never been a presbyter at all in the Catholic Church, nor has ever appeared as a presbyter in the assemblies of the Church; for not even when Alexander admitted those of the Meletian schism, by the indulgence of the great Council, was he named by Meletius among his presbyters, as they deposed; which is the strongest argument possible that he was not even a presbyter of Meletius; for otherwise, he would certainly have been numbered with the rest.

Besides, it was shewn also by Athanasius from the reports, that Ischyras had spoken falsely in other instances: for he set up a charge respecting the burning of certain books, when, as they pretend, Macarius burst in upon them, but was convicted of falsehood by the witnesses he himself brought to prove it.

29. Now when these things were thus represented to us, and so many witnesses appeared in his favour, and so much was advanced by him in his own justification, what did it become us to do? what did the rule of the Church require of us, but that we should not condemn him, but rather receive him and treat him like a Bishop, as we have done? Moreover, besides all this he continued here a year and six months, expecting the arrival of yourselves and of whoever chose to come, and by his presence he put everyone to shame, for he would not have been here, had he not felt confident in his cause; and he came not of his own accord, but on an invitation by letter from us, in the manner in which we wrote to you. But still you complain after all of our transgressing the Canons. Now consider; who are they that have so acted? we who received this man with such ample proof of his innocence, or they who, being at Antioch at the distance of six and thirty posts, nominated a stranger to be Bishop, and sent him to Alexandria with a military force; a thing which was not done even when Athanasius was banished into Gaul, though it would have been done then, had he

been really proved guilty of the offence. But when he returned, of course he found his Church unoccupied and waiting for him.

30. But now I am ignorant under what colour these proceedings have been carried on. In the first place, if the truth must be spoken, it was not right, when we had written to summon a council, that any persons should anticipate its decisions: and in the next place, it was not fitting that such novel proceedings should be adopted against the Church. For what canon of the Church, or what Apostolical tradition warrants this, that when a Church was at peace, and so many Bishops were in unanimity with Athanasius the Bishop of Alexandria, Gregory should be sent thither, a stranger to the city, not having been baptized there, nor known to the general body, and desired neither by Presbyters, nor Bishops, nor Laity–that he should be appointed at Antioch, and sent to Alexandria, accompanied not by presbyters, nor by deacons of the city, nor by bishops of Egypt, but by soldiers? for they who came hither complained that this was the case.

Even supposing that Athanasius was in the position of a criminal after the Council, this appointment ought not to have been made thus illegally and contrary to the rule of the Church, but the Bishops of the province ought to have ordained one in that very Church, of that very Priesthood, of that very Clergy; and the Canons received from the Apostles ought not thus to be set aside. Had this offence been committed against any one of you, would you not have exclaimed against it, and demanded justice as for the transgression of the Canons? Dearly beloved, we speak honestly, as in the presence of God, and declare, that this proceeding was neither pious, nor lawful, nor ecclesiastical. Moreover, the account which is given of the conduct of Gregory on his entry into the city, plainly shews the character of his appointment. In such peaceful times, as those who came from Alexandria declared them to have been, and as the Bishops also represented in their letters, the Church was set on fire; Virgins were stripped; Monks were trodden under foot; Presbyters and many of the people were scourged and suffered violence; Bishops were cast into prison; multitudes were dragged about from place to place; the holy Mysteries, about which they accused the Presbyter Macarius, were seized upon by heathens and cast upon the ground; and all to constrain certain persons to admit the appointment of Gregory. Such conduct plainly shews who they are that transgress the Canons. Had the appointment been lawful, he would not have had recourse to illegal proceedings to compel the obedience of those who in a legal way resisted him. And notwithstanding all this, you write that perfect peace prevailed in Alexandria and Egypt. Surely not, unless the work of peace is entirely changed, and you call such doings as these peace.

31. I have also thought it necessary to point out to you this circumstance, viz. that Athanasius positively asserted that Macarius was kept at Tyre under a guard of soldiers, while only his accuser accompanied those who went to the Mareotis; and that the Presbyters who desired to attend the inquiry were not permitted to do so, while the said inquiry respecting the cup and the Table was carried on before the Prefect and his band, and in the presence of Heathens and Jews. This at first seemed incredible, but it was proved to have been so from the Reports; which caused great astonishment to us, as I suppose, dearly beloved, it does to you also. Presbyters, who are the ministers of the Mysteries, are not permitted to attend, but an enquiry concerning Christ's Blood and Christ's Body is carried on before an external judge, in the presence of Catechumens, nay, worse than that, before Heathens and Jews, who are in ill repute in regard to Christianity. Even supposing that an offense had been committed, it should have been investigated legally in the Church and by the Clergy, not by heathens who abhor the Word and know not the Truth. I am persuaded that both you and all men must perceive the nature and magnitude of this sin. Thus much concerning Athanasius.

32. With respect to Marcellus, forasmuch as you have charged him also of impiety towards Christ, I am anxious to inform you, that when he was here, he positively declared that what you had written

concerning him was not true; but being nevertheless requested by us to give an account of his faith, he answered in his own person with the utmost boldness, so that we recognised that he maintains nothing outside the truth. He made a confession of the same godly doctrines concerning our Lord and Saviour Jesus Christ as the Catholic Church confesses; and he affirmed that he had held these opinions for a very long time, and had not recently adopted them: as indeed our Presbyters, who were at a former date present at the Council of Nicaea, testified to his orthodoxy; for he maintained then, as he has done now, his opposition to Arianism (on which points it is right to admonish you, lest any of you admit such heresy, instead of abominating it as alien from sound doctrine). Seeing then that he professed orthodox opinions, and had testimony to his orthodoxy, what, I ask again in his case, ought we to have done, except to receive him as a Bishop, as we did, and not reject him from our communion? These things I have written, not so much for the purpose of defending their cause, as in order to convince you, that we acted justly and canonically in receiving these persons, and that you are contentious without a cause. But it is your duty to use your anxious endeavours and to labour by every means to correct the irregularities which have been committed contrary to the Canon, and to secure the peace of the Churches; so that the peace of our Lord which has been given to us may remain, and the Churches may not be divided, nor you incur the charge of being authors of schism. For I confess, your past conduct is an occasion of schism rather than of peace.

33. For not only the Bishops Athanasius and Marcellus and their fellows came hither and complained of the injustice that had been done them, but many other Bishops also, from Thrace, from Coele-Syria, from Phoenicia and Palestine, and Presbyters, not a few, and others from Alexandria and from other parts, were present at the Council here, and in addition to their other statements, lamented before all the assembled Bishops the violence and injustice which the Churches had suffered, and affirmed that similar outrages to those which had been committed in Alexandria had occurred in their own Churches, and in others also. Again there lately came Presbyters with letters from Egypt and Alexandria, who complained that many Bishops and Presbyters who wished to come to the Council were prevented; for they said that, since the departure of Athanasius even up to this time, Bishops who are confessors have been beaten with stripes, that others have been cast into prison, and that but lately aged men, who have been an exceedingly long period in the Episcopate, have been given up to be employed in the public works, and nearly all the Clergy of the Catholic Church with the people are the objects of plots and persecutions. Moreover they said that certain Bishops and other brethren had been banished for no other reason than to compel them against their will to communicate

with Gregory and his Arian associates. We have heard also from others, what is confirmed by the testimony of the Bishop Marcellus, that a number of outrages, similar to those which were committed at Alexandria, have occurred also at Ancyra in Galatia. And in addition to all this, those who came to the Council reported against some of you (for I will not mention names) certain charges of so dreadful a nature that I have declined setting them down in writing: perhaps you also have heard them from others. It was for this cause especially that I wrote to desire you to come, that you might be present to hear them, and that all irregularities might be corrected and differences healed. And those who were called for these purposes ought not to have refused, but to have come the more readily, lest by failing to do so they should be suspected of what was alleged against them, and be thought unable to prove what they had written.

34. Now according to these representations, since the Churches are thus afflicted and treacherously assaulted, as our informants positively affirmed, who are they that have lighted up a flame of discord? We, who grieve for such a state of things and sympathize with the sufferings of the brethren, or they who have brought these things about? While then such extreme confusion existed in every Church, which was the cause why those who visited us came hither, I wonder how you could write that unanimity prevailed in the Churches. These things tend not to

the edification of the Church, but to her destruction; and those who rejoice in them are not sons of peace, but of confusion: but our God is not a God of confusion, but of peace. Wherefore, as the God and Father of our Lord Jesus Christ knows, it was from a regard for your good name, and with prayers that the Churches might not fall into confusion, but might continue as they were regulated by the Apostles, that I thought it necessary to write thus unto you, to the end that you might at length put to shame those who through the effects of their mutual enmity have brought the Churches to this condition. For I have heard, that it is only a certain few who are the authors of all these things.

Now, as having bowels of mercy, take ye care to correct, as I said before, the irregularities which have been committed contrary to the Canon, so that if any mischief has already befallen, it may be healed through your zeal. And write not that I have preferred the communion of Marcellus and Athanasius to yours, for such like complaints are no indications of peace, but of contentiousness and hatred of the brethren. For this cause I have written the foregoing, that you may understand that we acted not unjustly in admitting them to our communion, and so may cease this strife. If you had come hither, and they had been condemned, and had appeared unable to produce reasonable evidence in support of their cause, you would have done well in writing thus. But seeing that, as I said before, we acted agreeably to the Canon, and not unjustly, in holding communion with them, I beseech you for the sake of Christ, suffer not the members of Christ to be torn asunder, neither trust to prejudices, but seek rather the peace of the Lord. It is neither holy nor just, in order to gratify the petty feeling of a few persons, to reject those who have never been condemned and thereby to grieve the Spirit. But if you think that you are able to prove anything against them, and to confute them face to face let those of you who please come hither: for they also promised that they would be ready to establish completely the truth of those things which they have reported to us.

35. Give us notice therefore of this, dearly beloved, that we may write both to them, and to the Bishops who will have again to assemble, so that the accused may be condemned in the presence of all, and confusion no longer prevail in the Churches. What has already taken place is enough: it is enough surely that Bishops have been sentenced to banishment in the presence of Bishops; of which it behoves me not to speak at length, lest I appear to press too heavily on those who were present on those occasions. But if one must speak the truth, matters ought not to have proceeded so far; their petty feeling ought not to have been suffered to reach the present pitch. Let us grant the "removal," as you write, of Athanasius and Marcellus, from their own places, yet what must one say of the case of the other Bishops and Presbyters who, as I said before, came hither from various parts,

and who complained that they also had been forced away, and had suffered the like injuries? O beloved, the decisions of the Church are no longer according to the Gospel, but tend only to banishment and death. Supposing, as you assert, that some offence rested upon those persons, the case ought to have been conducted against them, not after this manner, but according to the Canon of the Church. Word should have been written of it to us all, that so a just sentence might proceed from all. For the sufferers were Bishops, and Churches of no ordinary note, but those which the Apostles themselves had governed in their own persons.

And why was nothing said to us concerning the Church of the Alexandrians in particular? Are you ignorant that the custom has been for word to be written first to us, and then for a just decision to be passed from this place? If then any such suspicion rested upon the Bishop there, notice thereof ought to have been sent to the Church of this place; whereas, after neglecting to inform us, and proceeding on their own authority as they pleased, now they desire to obtain our concurrence in their decisions, though we never condemned him. Not so have the constitutions of Paul, not so have the traditions of the Fathers directed; this is another form of procedure, a novel practice. I beseech you, readily bear with me: what I write is for the common good. For what we have received from the blessed Apostle Peter, that I signify to you; and I should not have written this, as deeming that these things were manifest unto all men, had not these proceedings so disturbed us. Bishops are forced away from their sees and driven into banishment, while others from different quarters are appointed in their place; others are treacherously assailed, so that the people have to grieve for those who are forcibly taken from them, while, as to those who are sent in their room, they are obliged to give over seeking the man whom they desire, and to receive those they do not.

I ask of you, that such things may no longer be, but that you will denounce in writing those persons who attempt them; so that the Churches may no longer be afflicted thus, nor any Bishop or Presbyter be treated with insult, nor any one be compelled to act contrary to his judgment, as they have represented to us, lest we become a laughing-stock among the heathen, and above all, lest we excite the wrath of God against us. For every one of us shall give account in the Day of judgment of the things which he has done in this life. May we all be possessed with the mind of God! so that the Churches may recover their own Bishops, and rejoice evermore in Jesus Christ our Lord; through Whom to the Father be glory, for ever and ever. Amen. I pray for your health in the Lord, brethren dearly beloved and greatly longed for.

36. Thus wrote the Council of Rome by Julius, Bishop of Rome.

Chapter 3

Letters of the Council of Sardica to the Churches of Egypt and of Alexandria, and to all Churches.

Letter of the Council of Sardica to the Church of Alexandria.

The Holy Council, by the grace of God assembled at Sardica, from Rome, Spain, Gaul, Italy, Campania, Calabria, Apulia, Africa, Sardinia, Pannonia, Moesia, Dacia, Noricum, Siscia, Dardania, the other Dacia, Macedonia, Thessaly, Achaia, Epirus, Thrace, Rhodope, Palestine, Arabia, Crete, and Egypt, to their beloved brothers, the Presbyters and Deacons, and to all the Holy Church of God abiding at Alexandria, sends health in the Lord.

37. We were not ignorant, but the fact was well known to us, even before we received the letters of your piety, that the supporters of the abominated heresy of the Arians were practising many dangerous machinations, rather to the destruction of their own souls, than to the injury of the Church. For this has ever been the object of their unprincipled craft; this is the deadly design in which they have been continually engaged; viz. how they may best expel from their places and persecute all who are to be found anywhere of orthodox sentiments, and maintaining the doctrine of the Catholic Church, which was delivered to them from the Fathers.

Against some they have laid false accusations; others they have driven into banishment; others they have destroyed by the punishments inflicted on them. At any rate they endeavoured by violence and tyranny to surprise the innocence of our brother and fellow-Bishop Athanasius, and therefore conducted their enquiry into his case without any care, without any faith, without any sort of justice. Accordingly having no confidence in the part they had played on that occasion, nor yet in the reports they had circulated against him, but perceiving that they were unable to produce any certain evidence respecting the case, when they came to the city of Sardica, they were unwilling to meet the Council of all the holy Bishops. From this it became evident that the decision of our brother and fellow-Bishop Julius was a just one; for after cautious deliberation and care he had determined, that we ought not to hesitate at all about communion with our brother Athanasius. For he had the credible testimony of eighty Bishops, and was also able to advance this fair argument in his support that by the mere means of our dearly beloved brethren his own Presbyters, and by correspondence, he had defeated the design of Eusebius and his fellows, who relied more upon violence than upon a judicial enquiry.

Wherefore all the Bishops from all parts determined upon holding communion with Athanasius on the ground that he was innocent. And let your charity also observe, that when he came to the holy Council assembled at Sardica, the Bishops of the East were informed of the circumstance, as we said before, both by letter, and by injunctions conveyed by word of mouth, and were invited by us to be present. But, being condemned by their own conscience, they had recourse to unbecoming excuses, and set themselves to avoid the enquiry. They demanded that an innocent man should be rejected from our communion, as a culprit, not considering how unbecoming, or rather how impossible, such a proceeding was. And as for the Reports which were framed in the Mareotis by certain most wicked and most abandoned youths, to whose hands one would not commit the very lowest office of the ministry, it is certain that they were ex parte statements. For neither was our brother the Bishop Athanasius present on the occasion, nor the Presbyter Macarius who was accused by them. And besides, their enquiry, or rather their falsification of facts, was attended by the most disgraceful circumstances. Sometimes heathens, sometimes Catechumens, were examined, not that they might declare what they knew, but that they might assert those falsehoods which they had been taught by others. And when you Presbyters, who were in charge in the absence of your Bishop, desired to be present at the enquiry, in order that you might shew the truth, and disprove the falsehoods, no regard was paid to you; they would not permit you to be present, but drove you away with insult.

Now although their calumnies have been most plainly exposed before all men by these circumstances; yet we found also, on reading the Reports, that the most iniquitous Ischyras, who has obtained from them the empty title of Bishop as his reward for the false accusation, had convicted himself of calumny. He declares in the Reports that at the very time when, according to his positive assertions, Macarius entered his cell, he lay there sick; whereas Eusebius and his fellows had the boldness to write that Ischyras was standing up and offering when Macarius came in.

38. The base and slanderous charge which they next alleged against him, has become well-known to all men. They raised a great outcry, affirming that Athanasius had committed murder, and had made away with one Arsenius a Meletian Bishop, whose loss they pretended to deplore with feigned lamentations and fictitious tears, and demanded that the body of a living man, as if a dead one, should be given up to them. But their fraud was not undetected; one and all knew that the person was alive, and was numbered among the living. And when these men, who are ready upon any opportunity, perceived their falsehoods detected (for Arsenius shewed himself alive, and so proved that he had not been made away with, and was not dead), yet they would not rest, but proceeded to add other to their former calumnies, and to slander the man by a fresh expedient. Well; our brother Athanasius,

dearly beloved, was not confounded, but again in the present case also with great boldness challenged them to the proof, and we too prayed and exhorted them to come to the trial, and if they were able, to establish their charge against him. O great arrogance! O dreadful pride! or rather, if one must say the truth, O evil and accusing conscience! for this is the view which all men take of it. Wherefore, beloved brethren, we admonish and exhort you, above all things to maintain the right faith of the Catholic Church. You have undergone many severe and grievous trials; many are the insults and injuries which the Catholic Church has suffered, but he that endureth to the end, the same shall be saved.'

Wherefore even though they still recklessly assail you, let your tribulation be unto you for joy. For such afflictions are a sort of martyrdom, and such confessions and tortures as yours will not be without their reward, but ye shall receive the prize from God. Therefore strive above all things in support of the sound faith, and of the innocence of your Bishop and our fellow-minister Athanasius. We also have not held our peace, nor been negligent of what concerns your comfort, but have deliberated and done whatsoever the claims of charity demand. We sympathize with our suffering brethren, and their affliction we consider as our own.

39. Accordingly we have written to beseech our most religious and godly Emperors, that their kindness

would give orders for the release of those who are still suffering from affliction and oppression, and would command that none of the magistrates, whose duty it is to attend only to civil causes, give judgment upon Clergy, nor henceforward in any way, on pretence of providing for the Churches, attempt anything against the brethren; but that every one may live, as he prays and desires to do, free from persecution, from violence and fraud, and in quietness and peace may follow the Catholic and Apostolic Faith. As for Gregory, who has the reputation of being illegally appointed by the heretics, and has been sent by them to your city, we wish your unanimity to understand, that he has been deposed by a judgment of the whole sacred Council, although indeed he has never at any time been considered to be a Bishop at all. Wherefore receive gladly your Bishop Athanasius, for to this end we have dismissed him in peace. And we exhort all those who either through fear, or through the intrigues of certain persons, have held communion with Gregory, that now being admonished, exhorted, and persuaded by us, they withdraw from that his detestable communion, and straightway unite themselves to the Catholic Church.

40. But forasmuch as we have learnt that Aphthonius, Athanasius the son of Capito, Paul, and Plutio, our fellow Presbyters, have also suffered from the machinations of Eusebius and his fellows, so that some of them have had trial of exile, and others have

fled on peril of their lives, we have in consequence thought it necessary to make this known unto you, that you may understand that we have received and acquitted them also, being aware that whatever has been done by Eusebius and his fellows against the orthodox has tended to the glory and commendation of those who have been attacked by them. It were fitting that your Bishop and our brother Athanasius should make this known to you respecting them, to his own respecting his own; but as for more abundant testimony he wished the holy Council also to write to you, we deferred not to do so, but hastened to signify this unto you, that you may receive them as we have done, for they also are deserving of praise, because through their piety towards Christ they have been thought worthy to endure violence at the hands of the heretics.

What decrees have been passed by the holy Council against those who are at the head of the Arian heresy, and have offended against you, and the rest of the Churches, you will learn from the subjoined documents. We have sent them to you, that you may understand from them that the Catholic Church will not overlook those who offend against her.

Letter of the Council of Sardica to the Bishops of Egypt and Libya.

The holy Council, by the grace of God assembled at Sardica, to the Bishops of Egypt and Libya, their fellow-ministers and dearly beloved brethren, sends health in the Lord.

41. We were not ignorant, but the fact was well known to us, even before we received the letters of your piety, that the supporters of the abominated heresy of the Arians were practising many dangerous machinations, rather to the destruction of their own souls, than to the injury of the Church. For this has ever been the object of their craft and villainy: this is the deadly design in which they have been continually engaged, viz. how they may best expel from their places and persecute all who are to be found anywhere of orthodox sentiments, and maintaining the doctrine of the Catholic Church, which was delivered to them from the Fathers. Against some they have laid false accusations; others they have driven into banishment; others they have destroyed by the punishments inflicted on them. At any rate they endeavoured by violence and tyranny to surprise the innocence of our brother and fellow-Bishop Athanasius, and therefore conducted their enquiry into his case without any faith, without any sort of justice. Accordingly having no confidence in the part they had played on that occasion, nor yet in the reports they had circulated against him, but perceiving that they were unable to produce any certain evidence respecting the case, when they came to the city of Sardica, they were unwilling to meet the Council of all the holy Bishops. From this it became evident that the decision of our brother and

fellow-Bishop Julius was a just one; for after cautious deliberation and care he had decided, that we ought not to hesitate at all about communion with our brother Athanasius. For he had the credible testimony of eighty Bishops, and was also able to advance this fair argument in his support, that by the mere means of our dearly beloved brethren his own Presbyters, and by correspondence, he had defeated the designs of Eusebius and his fellows, who relied more upon violence than upon a judicial inquiry.

Wherefore all the Bishops from all parts determined upon holding communion with Athanasius on the ground that he was innocent. And let your charity also observe, that when he came to the holy Council assembled at Sardica, the Bishops of the East were informed of the circumstance, as we said before, both by letter, and by injunctions conveyed by word of mouth, and were invited by us to be present. But, being condemned by their own conscience, they had recourse to unbecoming excuses, and began to avoid the enquiry. They demanded that an innocent man should be rejected from our communion, as a culprit, not considering how unbecoming, or rather how impossible, such a proceeding was. And as for the reports which were framed in the Mareotis by certain most wicked and abandoned youths, to whose hands one would not commit the very lowest office of the ministry, it is certain that they were ex parte statements. For neither was our brother the Bishop Athanasius present on the occasion, nor the

Presbyter Macarius, who was accused by them. And besides, their enquiry, or rather their falsification of facts, was attended by the most disgraceful circumstances. Sometimes Heathens, sometimes Catechumens, were examined, not that they might declare what they knew, but that they might assert those falsehoods which they had been taught by others. And when you Presbyters, who were in charge in the absence of your Bishop, desired to be present at the enquiry, in order that you might shew the truth, and disprove falsehood, no regard was paid to you; they would not permit you to be present, but drove you away with insult.

Now although their calumnies have been most plainly exposed before all men by these circumstances; yet we found also, on reading the Reports, that the most iniquitous Ischyras, who has obtained from them the empty title of Bishop as his reward for the false accusation, had convicted himself of calumny. He declares in the Reports, that at the very time when, according to his positive assertions, Macarius entered his cell, he lay there sick; whereas Eusebius and his fellows had the boldness to write that Ischyras was standing offering when Macarius came in.

42. The base and slanderous charge which they next alleged against him has become well known unto all men. They raised a great outcry, affirming that Athanasius had committed murder, and made away

with one Arsenius a Meletian Bishop, whose loss they pretended to deplore with feigned lamentations, and fictitious tears, and demanded that the body of a living man, as if a dead one, should be given up to them. But their fraud was not undetected; one and all knew that the person was alive, and was numbered among the living. And when these men, who are ready upon any opportunity, perceived their falsehood detected (for Arsenius shewed himself alive, and so proved that he had not been made away with, and was not dead), yet they would not rest, but proceeded to add other to their former calumnies, and to slander the man by a fresh expedient. Well: our brother Athanasius, dearly beloved, was not confounded, but again in the present case also with great boldness challenged them to the proof, and we too prayed and exhorted them to come to the trial, and if they were able, to establish their charge against him. O great arrogance! O dreadful pride! or rather, if one must say the truth, O evil and accusing conscience! for this is the view which all men take of it.

Wherefore, beloved brethren, we admonish and exhort you, above all things, to maintain the right faith of the Catholic Church. You have undergone many severe and grievous trials; many are the insults and injuries which the Catholic Church has suffered, but he that endureth to the end, the same shall be saved.' Wherefore, even though they shall still recklessly assail you, let your tribulation be unto you for joy. For such afflictions are a sort of martyrdom, and such confessions and tortures as yours will not be without their reward, but ye shall receive the prize from God. Therefore strive above all things in support of the sound Faith, and of the innocence of your Bishop and our brother Athanasius. We also have not held our peace, nor been negligent of what concerns your comfort, but have deliberated and done whatsoever the claims of charity demand. We sympathize with our suffering brethren, and their afflictions we consider as our own, and have mingled our tears with yours. And you, brethren, are not the only persons who have suffered: many others also of our brethren in ministry have come hither, bitterly lamenting these things.

43. Accordingly, we have written to beseech our most religious and godly Emperors, that their kindness would give orders for the release of those who are still suffering from affliction and oppression, and would command that none of the magistrates, whose duty it is to attend only to civil causes, give judgment upon Clergy, nor henceforward in any way, on pretence of providing for the Churches, attempt anything against the brethren, but that every one may live, as he prays and desires to do, free from persecution, from violence and fraud, and in quietness and peace may follow the Catholic and Apostolic Faith. As for Gregory, who has the reputation of being illegally appointed by the heretics, and who has been sent by them to your city,

we wish your unanimity to understand, that he has been deposed by the judgment of the whole sacred Council, although indeed he has never at any time been considered to be a Bishop at all. Wherefore receive gladly your Bishop Athanasius; for to this end we have dismissed him in peace. And we exhort all those, who either through fear, or through intrigues of certain persons, have held communion with Gregory, that being now admonished, exhorted, and persuaded by us, they withdraw from his detestable communion, and straightway unite themselves to the Catholic Church.

What decrees have been passed by the holy Council against Theodorus, Narcissus, Stephanus, Acacius, Menophantus, Ursacius, Valens, and George, who are the heads of the Arian heresy, and have offended against you and the rest of the Churches, you will learn from the subjoined documents. We have sent them to you, that your piety may assent to our decisions, and that you may understand from them, that the Catholic Church will not overlook those who offend against her.

Encyclical Letter of the Council of Sardica.

The holy Council, by the grace of God, assembled at Sardica, to their dearly beloved brethren, the Bishops and fellow-Ministers of the Catholic Church every where, sends health in the Lord.

44. The Arian madmen have dared repeatedly to attack the servants of God, who maintain the right faith; they attempted to substitute a spurious doctrine, and to drive out the orthodox; and at last they made so violent an assault against the Faith, that it became known even to the piety of our most religious Emperors. Accordingly, the grace of God assisting them, our most religious Emperors have themselves assembled us together out of different provinces and cities, and have permitted this holy Council to be held in the city of Sardica; to the end that all dissension may be done away, and all false doctrine being driven from us, Christian godliness may alone be maintained by all men. The Bishops of the East also attended, being exhorted to do so by the most religious Emperors, chiefly on account of the reports they have so often circulated concerning our dearly beloved brethren and fellow-ministers Athanasius, Bishop of Alexandria, and Marcellus, Bishop of Ancyro-Galatia. Their calumnies have probably already reached you, and perhaps they have attempted to disturb your ears, that you may be induced to believe their charges against the innocent, and that they may obliterate from your minds any suspicions respecting their own wicked heresy. But they have not been permitted to effect this to any great extent; for the Lord is the Defender of His Churches, Who endured death for their sakes and for us all, and provided access to heaven for us all through Himself. When therefore Eusebius and his fellows wrote long ago to Julius our brother and

Bishop of the Church of the Romans, against our forementioned brethren, that is to say, Athanasius, Marcellus, and Asclepas, the Bishops from the other parts wrote also, testifying to the innocence of our fellow-minister Athanasius, and declaring that the representations of Eusebius and his fellows were nothing else but mere falsehood and calumny.

And indeed their calumnies were clearly proved by the fact that, when they were invited to a Council by our dearly beloved fellow-minister Julius, they would not come, and also by what was written to them by Julius himself. For had they had confidence in the measures and the acts in which they were engaged against our brethren, they would have come. And besides, they gave a still more evident proof of their conspiracy by their conduct in this great and holy Council. For when they arrived at the city of Sardica, and saw our brethren Athanasius, Marcellus, Asclepas, and the rest, they were afraid to come to a trial and though they were repeatedly invited to attend, they would not obey the summons. Although all we Bishops met together, and above all that man of most happy old age, Hosius, one who on account of his age, his confession, and the many labours he has undergone, is worthy of all reverence; and although we waited and urged them to come to the trial, that in the presence of our fellow-ministers they might establish the truth of those charges which they had circulated and written against them in their absence; yet they would not come, when they were thus invited, as we said before, thus giving proof of their calumnies, and almost proclaiming to the world by this their refusal, the plot and conspiracy in which they have been engaged. They who are confident of the truth of their assertions are able to make them good against their opponents face to face. But as they would not meet us, we think that no one can now doubt, however they may again have recourse to their bad practices, that they possess no proof against our fellow-ministers, but calumniate them in their absence, while they avoid their presence.

45. They fled, beloved brethren, not only on account of the calumnies they had uttered, but because they saw that those had come who had various charges to advance against them. For chains and irons were brought forward which they had used; persons appeared who had returned from banishment; there came also our brethren, kinsmen of those who were still detained in exile, and friends of such as had perished through their means. And what was the most weighty ground of accusation, Bishops were present, one of whom brought forward the irons and chains which they had caused him to wear, and others appealed to the death which had been brought about by their calumnies. For they had proceeded to such a pitch of madness, as even to attempt to destroy Bishops; and would have destroyed them, had they not escaped their hands. Our fellow-ministers, Theodulus of blessed memory, died during his flight from their false accusations, orders

having been given in consequence of these to put him to death. Others also exhibited sword-wounds; and others complained that they had been exposed to the pains of hunger through their means. Nor were they ordinary persons who testified to these things, but whole Churches, in whose behalf legates appeared, and told us of soldiers sword in hand, of multitudes armed with clubs, of the threats of judges, of the forgery of false letters. For there were read certain false letters of Theognius and his fellows against our fellow-ministers Athanasius, Marcellus, and Asclepas, written with the design of exasperating the Emperors against them; and those who had then been Deacons of Theognius proved the fact. From these men, we heard of virgins stripped naked, churches burnt, ministers in custody, and all for no other end, but only for the sake of the accursed heresy of the Arian madmen, whose communion whoso refused was forced to suffer these things.

When they perceived then how matters lay, they were in a strait what course to choose. They were ashamed to confess what they had done, but were unable to conceal it any longer. They therefore came to the city of Sardica, that by their arrival they might seem to remove suspicion from themselves of such offences. But when they saw those whom they had calumniated, and those who had suffered at their hands; when they had before their eyes their accusers and the proofs of their guilt, they were unwilling to come forward, though invited by our fellow-ministers Athanasius, Marcellus, and Asclepas, who with great freedom complained of their conduct, and urged and challenged them to the trial, promising not only to refute their calumnies, but also to bring proof of the offences which they had committed against their Churches. But they were seized with such terrors of conscience, that they fled; and in doing so they exposed their own calumnies and confessed by running away the offences of which they had been guilty.

46. But although their malice and their calumnies have been plainly manifested on this as well as on former occasions, yet that they may not devise means of practising a further mischief in consequence of their flight, we have considered it advisable to examine the part they have played according to the principles of truth; this has been our purpose, and we have found them calumniators by their acts, and authors of nothing else than a plot against our brethren in ministry. For Arsenius, who they said had been murdered by Athanasius, is still alive, and is numbered among the living; from which we may infer that the reports they have spread abroad on other subjects are fabrications also. And whereas they spread abroad a rumour concerning a cup, which they said had been broken by Macarius the Presbyter of Athanasius, those who came from Alexandria, the Mareotis, and the other parts, testified that nothing of the kind had taken place. And the Egyptian Bishops who wrote to Julius our fellow-minister,

positively affirmed that there had not arisen among them even any suspicion whatever of such a thing.

Moreover, the Reports, which they say they have to produce against him, are, as is notorious, ex parte statements; and even in the formation of these very Reports, Heathens and Catechumens were examined; one of whom, a Catechumen, said in his examination that he was present in the room when Macarius broke in upon them; and another declared, that Ischyras of whom they speak so much, lay sick in his cell at the time; from which it appears that the Mysteries were never celebrated at all, because Catechumens were present, and also that Ischyras was not present, but was lying sick on his bed. Besides, this most worthless Ischyras, who has falsely asserted, as he was convicted of doing, that Athanasius had burnt some of the sacred books, has himself confessed that he was sick, and was lying in his bed when Macarius came; from which it is plain that he is a slanderer. Nevertheless, as a reward for these his calumnies, they have given to this very Ischyras the title of Bishop, although he is not even a Presbyter. For two Presbyters, who were once associated with Meletius, but were afterwards received by the blessed Alexander, Bishop of Alexandria, and are now with Athanasius, appeared before the Council, and testified that he was not even a Presbyter of Meletius, and that Meletius never had either Church or Minister in the Mareotis. And yet this man, who has never been even a Presbyter, they have now brought forward as a Bishop, that by this name they may have the means of overpowering those who are within hearing of his calumnies.

47. The book of our fellow-minister Marcellus was also read, by which the fraud of Eusebius and his fellows was plainly discovered. For what Marcellus had advanced by way of enquiry, they falsely represented as his professed opinion; but when the subsequent parts of the book were read, and the parts preceding the queries themselves, his faith was found to be correct. He had never pretended, as they positively affirmed, that the Word of God had His beginning from holy Mary, nor that His kingdom had an end; on the contrary he had written that His kingdom was both without beginning and without end. Our fellow-minister Asclepas also produced Reports which had been drawn up at Antioch in the presence of his accusers and Eusebius of Caesarea, and proved that he was innocent by the declarations of the Bishops who judged his cause. They had good reason therefore, dearly beloved brethren, for not hearkening to our frequent summons, and for deserting the Council. They were driven to this by their own consciences; but their flight only confirmed the proof of their own calumnies, and caused those things to be believed against them, which their accusers, who were present, were asserting and arguing. But besides all these things, they had not only received those who were formerly degraded and ejected on account of the heresy of

Arius, but had even promoted them to a higher station, advancing Deacons to the Presbytery, and of Presbyters making Bishops, for no other end, but that they might disseminate and spread abroad impiety, and corrupt the orthodox faith.

48. Their leaders are now, after Eusebius and his fellows, Theodorus of Heraclea, Narcissus of Neronias in Cilicia, Stephanus of Antioch, George of Laodicea, Acacius of Caesarea in Palestine, Menophantus of Ephesus in Asia, Ursacius of Singidunum in Moesia, and Valens of Mursa in Pannonia. These men would not permit those who came with them from the East to meet the holy Council, nor even to approach the Church of God; but as they were coming to Sardica, they held Councils in various places by themselves, and made an engagement under threats, that when they came to Sardica, they would not so much as appear at the trial, nor attend the assembling of the holy Council, but simply coming and making known their arrival as a matter of form, would speedily take to flight. This we have been able to ascertain from our fellow-ministers, Macarius of Palestine and Asterius of Arabia, who after coming in their company, separated themselves from their unbelief. These came to the holy Council, and complained of the violence they had suffered, and said that no right act was being done by them; adding that there were many among them who adhered to orthodoxy, but were prevented by those men from coming hither, by

means of the threats and promises which they held out to those who wished to separate from them. On this account it was that they were so anxious that all should abide in one dwelling, and would not suffer them to be by themselves even for the shortest space of time.

49. Since then it became us not to hold our peace, nor to pass over unnoticed their calumnies, imprisonments, murders, wounds, conspiracies by means of false letters, outrages, stripping of the virgins, banishments, destruction of the Churches, burnings, translations from small cities to larger dioceses, and above all, the rising of the ill-named Arian heresy by their means against the orthodox faith; we have therefore pronounced our dearly beloved brethren and fellow-ministers Athanasius, Marcellus, and Asclepas, and those who minister to the Lord with them, to be innocent and clear of offence, and have written to the diocese of each, that the people of each Church may know the innocence of their own Bishop, and may esteem him as their Bishop and expect his coming.

And as for those who like wolves have invaded their Churches, Gregory at Alexandria, Basil at Ancyra, and Quintianus at Gaza, let them neither give them the title of Bishop, nor hold any communion at all with them, nor receive letters from them, nor write to them. And for Theodorus, Narcissus, Acacius, Stephanus, Ursacius, Valens, Menophantus, and

George, although the last from fear did not come from the East, yet because he was deposed by the blessed Alexander, and because both he and the others were connected with the Arian madness, as well as on account of the charges which lie against them, the holy Council has unanimously deposed them from the Episcopate, and we have decided that they not only are not Bishops, but that they are unworthy of holding communion with the faithful.

For they who separate the Son and alienate the Word from the Father, ought themselves to be separated from the Catholic Church and to be alien from the Christian name. Let them therefore be anathema to you, because they have corrupted the word of truth.' It is an Apostolic injunction, If any man preach any other Gospel unto you than that ye have received, let him be accursed.' Charge your people that no one hold communion with them, for there is no communion of light with darkness; put away from you all these, for there is no concord of Christ in Belial. And take heed, dearly beloved, that ye neither write to them, nor receive letters from them; but desire rather, brethren and fellow-ministers, as being present in spirit with our Council, to assent to our judgments by your subscriptions, to the end that concord may be preserved by all our fellow-ministers everywhere. May Divine Providence protect and keep you, dearly beloved brethren, in sanctification and joy.

I, Hosius, Bishop, have subscribed this, and all the rest likewise. This is the letter which the Council of Sardica sent to those who were unable to attend, and they on the other hand gave their judgment in accordance; and the following are the names both of those Bishops who subscribed in the Council, and of the others also.

50. Hosius of Spain, Julius of Rome by his Presbyters Archidamus and Philoxenus, Protogenes of Sardica, Gaudentius, Macedonius, Severus, Praetextatus, Ursicius, Lucillus, Eugenius, Vitalius, Calepodius, Florentius, Bassus, Vincentius, Stercorius, Palladius, Domitianus, Chalbis, Gerontius, Protasius, Eulogus, Porphyrius, Dioscorus, Zosimus, Januarius, Zosimus, Alexander, Eutychius, Socrates, Diodorus, Martyrius, Eutherius, Eucarpus, Athenodorus, Irenaeus, Julianus, Alypius, Jonas, Aetius, Restitutus, Marcellinus, Aprianus, Vitalius, Valens, Hermogenes, Castus, Domitianus, Fortunatius, Marcus, Annianus, Heliodorus, Musaeus, Asterius, Paregorius, Plutarchus, Hymenaeus, Athanasius, Lucius, Amantius, Arius, Asclepius, Dionysius, Maximus, Tryphon, Alexander, Antigonus, AElianus, Petrus, Symphorus, Musonius, Eutychus, Philologius, Spudasius, Zosimus, Patricius, Adolius, Sapricius.

From Gaul the following; Maximianus, Verissimus, Victurus, Valentinus, Desiderius, Eulogius, Sarbatius, Dyscolius, Superior, Mercurius,

Declopetus, Eusebius, Severinus, Satyrus, Martinus, Paulus, Optatianus, Nicasius, Victor, Sempronius, Valerinus, Pacatus, Jesses, Ariston, Simplicius, Metianus, Amantus, Amillianus, Justinianus, Victorinus, Satornilus, Abundantius, Donatianus, Maximus.

From Africa; Nessus, Gratus, Megasius, Coldaeus, Rogatianus, Consortius, Rufinus, Manninus, Cessilianus, Herennianus, Marianus, Valerius, Dynamius, Mizonius, Justus, Celestinus, Cyprianus, Victor, Honoratus, Marinus, Pantagathus, Felix, Baudius, Liber, Capito, Minervalis, Cosmus, Victor, Hesperio, Felix, Severianus, Optantius, Hesperus, Fidentius, Salustius, Paschasius.

From Egypt; Liburnius, Amantius, Felix, Ischyrammon, Romulus, Tiberinus, Consortius, Heraclides, Fortunatius, Dioscorus, Fortunatianus, Bastamon, Datyllus, Andreas, Serenus, Arius, Theodorus, Evagoras, Helias, Timotheus, Orion, Andronicus, Paphnutius, Hermias, Arabion, Psenosiris, Apollonius, Muis, Sarapampon [638] , Philo, Philippus, Apollonius, Paphnutius, Paulus, Dioscorus, Nilammon, Serenus, Aquila, Aotas, Harpocration, Isac, Theodorus, Apollos, Ammonianus, Nilus, Heraclius, Arion, Athas, Arsenius, Agathammon, Theon, Apollonius, Helias, Paninuthius, Andragathius, Nemesion, Sarapion, Ammonius, Ammonius, Xenon, Gerontius, Quintus, Leonides, Sempronianus, Philo, Heraclides,

Hieracys, Rufus, Pasophius, Macedonius, Apollodorus, Flavianus, Psaes, Syrus, Apphus, Sarapion, Esaias, Paphnutius, Timotheus, Elurion, Gaius, Musaeus, Pistus, Heraclammon, Heron, Helias, Anagamphus, Apollonius, Gaius, Philotas, Paulus, Tithoes, Eudaemon, Julius.

Those on the road of Italy are Probatius, Viator, Facundinus, Joseph, Numedius, Sperantius, Severus, Heraclianus, Faustinus, Antoninus, Heraclius, Vitalius, Felix, Crispinus, Paulianus. From Cyprus; Auxibius, Photius, Gerasius, Aphrodisius, Irenicus, Nunechius, Athanasius, Macedonius, Triphyllius, Spyridon, Norbanus, Sosicrates. From Palestine; Maximus, Aetius, Arius, Theodosius, Germanus, Silvanus, Paulus, Claudius, Patricius, Elpidius, Germanus, Eusebius, Zenobius, Paulus, Petrus. These are the names of those who subscribed to the acts of the Council; but there are very many beside, out of Asia, Phrygia, and Isauria, who wrote in my behalf before this Council was held, and whose names, nearly sixty-three in number, may be found in their own letters. They amount altogether to three hundred and forty-four.

Chapter 4

Imperial and Ecclesiastical Acts in Consequence of the Decision of the Council of Sardica.

51. When the most religious Emperor Constantius heard of these things, he sent for me, having written privately to his brother Constans of blessed memory, and to me three several times in the following terms.

Constantius Victor Augustus to Athanasius. Our benignant clemency will not suffer you to be any longer tempest-tossed by the wild waves of the sea; for our unwearied piety has not lost sight of you, while you have been bereft of your native home, deprived of your goods, and have been wandering in savage wildernesses. And although I have for a long time deferred expressing by letter the purpose of my mind concerning you, principally because I expected that you would appear before us of your own accord, and would seek a relief of your sufferings; yet forasmuch as fear, it may be, has prevented you from fulfilling your intentions, we have therefore addressed to your fortitude letters full of our bounty, to the end that you may use all speed and without fear present yourself in our presence, thereby to obtain the enjoyment of your wishes, and that, having experience of our kindness, you may be restored again to your own. For this purpose I have besought my lord and brother Constans Victor Augustus, in your behalf, that he would give you permission to come, in order that you may be restored to your country with the consent of us both, receiving this as a pledge of our favour.

The Second Letter.

Although we made it very plain to you in a former letter that you may without hesitation come to our Court, because we greatly wished to send you home, yet, we have further sent this present letter to your fortitude to exhort you without any distrust or apprehension, to place yourself in the public conveyances, and to hasten to us, that you may enjoy the fulfilment of your wishes.

The Third Letter.

Our pleasure was, while we abode at Edessa, and your Presbyters were there, that, on one of them being sent to you, you should make haste to come to our Court, in order that you might see our face, and straightway proceed to Alexandria. But as a very long period has elapsed since you received letters from us, and you have not yet come, we therefore hasten to remind you again, that you may endeavour even now to present yourself before us with speed, and so may be restored to your country, and obtain the accomplishment of your prayers. And for your fuller information we have sent Achitas the Deacon, from whom you will be able to learn the purpose of our soul, that you may now secure the objects of your prayers.

Such was the tenor of the Emperor's letters; on receiving which I went up to Rome to bid farewell to the Church and the Bishop: for I was at Aquileia when the above was written. The Church was filled with all joy, and the Bishop Julius rejoiced with me in my return and wrote to the Church; and as we passed along, the Bishops of every place sent us on our way in peace. The letter of Julius was as follows.

52. Julius to the Presbyters, Deacons, and people residing at Alexandria.

I congratulate you, beloved brethren, that you now behold the fruit of your faith before your eyes; for any one may see that such indeed is the case with respect to my brother and fellow-Bishop Athanasius, whom for the innocency of his life, and by reason of your prayers, God is restoring to you again. Wherefore it is easy to perceive, that you have continually offered up to God pure prayers and full of love. Being mindful of the heavenly promises, and of the conversation that leads to them, which you have learnt from the teaching of my brother aforesaid, you knew certainly and understood by the right faith that is in you, that he, whom you always had as present in your most pious minds, would not be separated from you for ever. Wherefore there is no need that I should use many words in writing to you; for your faith has already anticipated whatever I could say to you, and has by the grace of God procured the accomplishment of the common prayers of you all. Therefore, I repeat again, I congratulate you, because you have preserved your souls unconquered in the faith; and I also congratulate no less my brother Athanasius, in that, though he is enduring many afflictions, he has at no time been forgetful of your love and earnest desires towards him. For although for a season he seemed to be withdrawn from you in body, yet he has continued to live as always present with you in spirit.

53. Wherefore he returns to you now more illustrious than when he went away from you. Fire tries and purifies the precious materials, gold and silver: but how can one describe the worth of such a man, who, having passed victorious through the perils of so many tribulations, is now restored to you, being pronounced innocent not by our voice only, but by the voice of the whole Council? Receive therefore, beloved brethren, with all godly honour and rejoicing, your Bishop Athanasius, together with those who have been partners with him in so many labours. And rejoice that you now obtain the fulfilment of your prayers, after that in your salutary letter you have given meat and drink to your Pastor, who, so to speak, longed and thirsted after your godliness. For while he sojourned in a foreign land, you were his consolation; and you refreshed him during his persecutions by your most faithful minds

and spirits. And it delights me now to conceive and figure to my mind the joy of every one of you at his return, and the pious greetings of the concourse, and the glorious festivity of those that run to meet him. What a day will that be to you, when my brother comes back again, and your former sufferings terminate, and his much-prized and desired return inspires you all with an exhilaration of perfect joy! The like joy it is ours to feel in a very great degree, since it has been granted us by God, to be able to make the acquaintance of so eminent a man. It is fitting therefore that I should conclude my letter with a prayer. May Almighty God, and His Son our Lord and Saviour Jesus Christ, afford you continual grace, giving you a reward for the admirable faith which you displayed in your noble confession in behalf of your Bishop, that He may impart unto you and unto them that are with you, both here and hereafter, those better things, which the eye hath not seen, nor ear heard, neither hath entered into the heart of man, the things which God hath prepared for them that love Him,' through our Lord Jesus Christ, through Whom to Almighty God be glory for ever and ever. Amen. I pray, dearly beloved brethren, for your health and strength in the Lord.

54. The Emperor, when I came to him with these letters, received me kindly, and sent me forth to my country and Church addressing the following to the Bishops, Presbyters, and People.

Constantius, Victor, Maximus, Augustus, to the Bishops and Presbyters of the Catholic Church.

The most reverend Athanasius has not been deserted by the grace of God, but although for a brief season he was subjected to trial to which human nature is liable, he has obtained from the all-surveying Providence such an answer to his prayers as was meet, and is restored by the will of the Most High, and by our sentence, at once to his country and to the Church, over which by divine permission he presided. Wherefore, in accordance with this, it is fitting that it should be provided by our clemency, that all the decrees which have heretofore been passed against those who held communion with him, be now consigned to oblivion, and that all suspicions respecting them be henceforward set at rest, and that immunity, such as the Clergy who are associated with him formerly enjoyed, be duly confirmed to them. Moreover to our other acts of favour towards him we have thought good to add the following, that all persons of the sacred catalogue should understand, that an assurance of safety is given to all who adhere to him, whether Bishops, or other Clergy. And union with him will be a sufficient guarantee, in the case of any person, of an upright intention. For whoever, acting according to a better judgment and part, shall choose to hold communion with him, we order, in imitation of that Providence which has already gone before, that all such should have the advantage of the grace which by the will of the Most High is now offered to them from us. May God preserve you.

The Second Letter.

Constantius, Victor, Maximus, Augustus, to the people of the Catholic Church at Alexandria.

55. Having in view your welfare in all respects, and knowing that you have for a long time been deprived of episcopal superintendence, we have thought good to send back to you your Bishop Athanasius, a man known to all men for the uprightness that is in him, and for the good disposition of his personal character. Receive him, as you are wont to receive every one, in a suitable manner, and, using his advocacy as your succour in your prayers to God, endeavour to preserve continually that unanimity and peace according to the order of the Church which is at the same time becoming in you, and most advantageous for us. For it is not becoming that any dissension or faction should be raised among you, contrary to the prosperity of our times. We desire that this offence may be altogether removed from you, and we exhort you to continue stedfastly in your accustomed prayers, and to make him, as we said before, your advocate and helper towards God. So that, when this your determination, beloved, has influenced the prayers of all men, even those heathen who are still addicted to the false worship of idols may eagerly desire to come to the

knowledge of our sacred religion. Again therefore we exhort you to continue in these things, and gladly to receive your Bishop, who is sent back to you by the decree of the Most High, and by our decision, and determine to greet him cordially with all your soul and with all your mind. For this is what is both becoming in you, and agreeable to our clemency. In order that all occasions of disturbance and sedition may be taken away from those who are maliciously disposed, we have by letter commanded the magistrates who are among you to subject to the vengeance of the law all whom they find to be factious. Wherefore taking into consideration both these things, our decision in accordance with the will of the Most High, and our regard for you and for concord among you, and the punishment that awaits the disorderly, observe such things as are proper and suitable to the order of our sacred religion, and receiving the afore-mentioned Bishop with all reverence and honour, take care to offer up with him your prayers to God, the Father of all, in behalf of yourselves, and for the well-being of your whole lives.

56. Having written these letters, he also commanded that the decrees, which he had formerly sent out against me in consequence of the calumnies of Eusebius and his fellows, should be cancelled and struck out from the Orders of the Duke and the Prefect of Egypt; and Eusebius the Decurion was

sent to withdraw them from the Order-books. His letter on this occasion was as follows.

Constantius, Victor, Augustus, to Nestorius. (And in the same terms, to the Governors of Augustamnica, the Thebais, and Libya.)

Whatever Orders are found to have been passed heretofore, tending to the injury and dishonour of those who hold communion with the Bishop Athanasius, we wish them to be now erased. For we desire that whatever immunities his Clergy possessed before, they should again possess the same. And we wish this our Order to be observed, that when the Bishop Athanasius is restored to his Church, those who hold communion with him may enjoy the immunities which they have always enjoyed, and which the rest of the Clergy enjoy; so that they may have the satisfaction of being on an equal footing with others.

57. Being thus set forward on my journey, as I passed through Syria, I met with the Bishops of Palestine, who when they had called a Council at Jerusalem, received me cordially, and themselves also sent me on my way in peace, and addressed the following letter to the Church and the Bishops.

The Holy Council, assembled at Jerusalem, to the fellow-ministers in Egypt and Libya, and to the Presbyters, Deacons, and People at Alexandria, brethren beloved and greatly longed for, sends health in the Lord.

We cannot give worthy thanks to the God of all, dearly beloved, for the wonderful things which He has done at all times, and especially at this time for your Church, in restoring to you your pastor and lord, and our fellow-minister Athanasius. For who ever hoped that his eyes would see what you are now actually obtaining? Of a truth, your prayers have been heard by the God of all, Who cares for His Church, and has looked upon your tears and groans, and has therefore heard your petitions. For ye were as sheep scattered and fainting, not having a shepherd. Wherefore the true Shepherd, Who careth for His own sheep, has visited you from heaven, and has restored to you him whom you desire. Behold, we also, being ready to do all things for the peace of the Church, and being prompted by the same affection as yourselves, have saluted him before you; and communicating with you through him, we send you these greetings, and our offering of thanksgiving, that you may know that we also are united in the bond of love that joins you to him. You are bound to pray also for the piety of our most God-beloved Emperors, who, when they knew your earnest longings after him, and his innocency, determined to restore him to you with all honour. Wherefore receive him with uplifted hands, and take good heed that you offer up due thanksgiving on his behalf to God Who has bestowed these blessings upon you; so that you may continually rejoice with God and glorify our Lord, in Christ Jesus our Lord, through Whom to the Father be glory for ever. Amen.

I have set down here the names of those who subscribed this letter, although I have mentioned them before. They are these; Maximus, Aetius, Arius, Theodorus, Germanus, Silvanus, Paulus, Patricius, Elpidius, Germanus, Eusebius, Zenobius, Paulus, Macrinus, Petrus, Claudius.

58. When Ursacius and Valens saw all this, they forthwith condemned themselves for what they had done, and going up to Rome, confessed their crime, declared themselves penitent, and sought forgiveness, addressing the following letters to Julius, Bishop of ancient Rome, and to ourselves. Copies of them were sent to me from Paulinus, Bishop of Treveri.

A Translation from the Latin of a Letter to Julius, concerning the recantation of Ursacius and Valens.

Ursacius and Valens to the most blessed lord, pope Julius.

Whereas it is well known that we have heretofore in letters laid many grievous charges against the Bishop Athanasius, and whereas when we were corrected by the letters of your Goodness, we were unable to render an account of the statement we had made; we do now confess before your Goodness, and in the presence of all the Presbyters our brethren, that all the reports which have heretofore come to your hearing respecting the case of the aforesaid Athanasius, are falsehoods and fabrications, and are utterly inconsistent with his character. Wherefore we earnestly desire communion with the aforesaid Athanasius, especially since your Piety, with your characteristic generosity, has vouchsafed to pardon our error. But we also declare, that if at any time the Eastern Bishops, or even Athanasius himself, ungenerously should wish to bring us to judgment for this matter, we will not depart contrary to your judgment. And as for the heretic Arius and his supporters, who say that once the Son was not, and that the Son was made of that which was not, and who deny that Christ is God and the Son of God before the worlds, we anathematize them both now and for evermore, as also we have set forth in our former declaration at Milan. We have written this with our own hands, and we profess again, that we have renounced for ever, as we said before, the Arian heresy and its authors.

I Ursacius subscribed this my confession in person; and likewise I Valens.

Ursacius and Valens, Bishops, to their lord and brother, the Bishop Athanasius. Having an opportunity of sending by our brother and fellow Presbyter Musaeus, who is coming to your Charity, we salute you affectionately, beloved brother, through him, from Aquileia, and pray you, being as we trust in health, to read our letter. You will also give us confidence, if you will return to us an answer in writing. For know that we are at peace with you, and in communion with the Church, of which the salutation prefixed to this letter is a proof. May Divine Providence preserve you, my Lord, our beloved brother! Such were their letters, and such the sentence and the judgment of the Bishops in my behalf. But in order to prove that they did not act thus to ingratiate themselves, or under compulsion in any quarter, I desire, with your permission, to recount the whole matter from the beginning, so that you may perceive that the bishops wrote as they did with upright and just intentions, and that Ursacius and Valens, though they were slow to do so, at last confessed the truth.

Chapter 5

Documents connected with the charges of the Meletians against S. Athanasius.

59. Peter was Bishop among us before the persecution, and during the course of it he suffered martyrdom. When Meletius, who held the title of bishop in Egypt, was convicted of many crimes, and among the rest of offering sacrifice to idols, Peter deposed him in a general council of the bishops. Whereupon Meletius did not appeal to another council, or attempt to justify himself before those who should come after, but made a schism, so that they who espoused his cause are even yet called Meletians instead of Christians. He began immediately to revile the bishops, and made false accusations, first against Peter himself, and against his successor Achillas, and after Achillas, against Alexander. And he thus practised craftily, following the example of Absalom, to the end that, as he was disgraced by his deposition, he might by his calumnies mislead the simple. While Meletius was thus employed, the Arian heresy also had arisen. But in the Council of Nicaea, while the heresy was anathematized, and the Arians were cast out, the Meletians on whatever grounds (for it is not necessary now to mention the reason) were received. Five months however had not yet passed when, the blessed Alexander having died, the Meletians, who ought to have remained quiet, and to have been

grateful that they were received on any terms, like dogs unable to forget their vomit, were again troubling the Churches.

Upon learning this, Eusebius, who had the lead in the Arian heresy, sends and buys the Meletians with large promises, becomes their secret friend, and arranges with them for their assistance on any occasion when he might wish for it. At first he sent to me, urging me to admit Arius and his fellows to communion, and threatened me in his verbal communications, while in his letters he [merely] made a request. And when I refused, declaring that it was not right that those who had invented heresy contrary to the truth, and had been anathematized by the Ecumenical Council, should be admitted to communion, he caused the Emperor also, Constantine, of blessed memory, to write to me, threatening me, in case I should not receive Arius and his fellows, with those afflictions, which I have before undergone, and which I am still suffering. The following is a part of his letter. Syncletius and Gaudentius, officers of the palace, were the bearers of it.

Part of a Letter from the Emperor Constantine.

Having therefore knowledge of my will, grant free admission to all who wish to enter into the Church. For if I learn that you have hindered or excluded any who claim to be admitted into communion with the

Church, I will immediately send some one who shall depose you by my command, and shall remove you from your place.

60. When upon this I wrote and endeavoured to convince the Emperor, that that anti-Christian heresy had no communion with the Catholic Church, Eusebius forthwith, availing himself of the occasion which he had agreed upon with the Meletians, writes and persuades them to invent some pretext, so that, as they had practised against Peter and Achillas and Alexander, they might devise and spread reports against us also. Accordingly, after seeking for a long time, and finding nothing, they at last agree together, with the advice of Eusebius and his fellows, and fabricate their first accusation by means of Ision, Eudaemon, and Callinicus, respecting the linen vestments, to the effect that I had imposed a law upon the Egyptians, and had required its observance of them first. But when certain Presbyters of mine were found to be present, and the Emperor took cognizance of the matter, they were condemned (the Presbyters were Apis and Macarius), and the Emperor wrote, condemning Ision, and ordering me to appear before him. His letters were as follows.

Eusebius, having intelligence of this, persuades them to wait; and when I arrive, they next accuse Macarius of breaking the cup, and bring against me the most heinous accusation possible, viz. that, being an enemy of the Emperor, I had sent a purse of gold to one Philumenus. The Emperor therefore heard us on this charge also in Psammathia, when they, as usual, were condemned, and driven from the presence; and, as I returned, he wrote the following letter to the people.

Constantine, Maximus, Augustus, to the people of the Catholic Church at Alexandria.

61. Beloved brethren, I greet you well, calling upon God, Who is the chief witness of my intention, and on the Only-begotten, the Author of our Law, Who is Sovereign over the lives of all men, and Who hates dissensions. But what shall I say to you? That I am in good health? Nay, but I should be able to enjoy better health and strength, if you were possessed with mutual love one towards another, and had rid yourselves of your enmities, through which, in consequence of the storms excited by contentious men, we have left the haven of brotherly love. Alas! what perverseness is this! What evil consequences are produced every day by the tumult of envy which has been stirred up among you! Hence it is that evil reports have settled upon the people of God. Whither has the faith of righteousness departed? For we are so involved in the mists of darkness, not only through manifold errors, but through the faults of ungrateful men, that we bear with those who favour folly, and though we are aware of them, take no heed of those who set aside goodness and truth. What

strange inconsistency is this! We do not convict our enemies, but we follow the example of robbery which they set us, whereby the most pernicious errors, finding no one to oppose them, easily, if I may so speak, make a way for themselves. Is there no understanding among us, for the credit of our common nature, since we are thus neglectful of the injunctions of the law?

But some one will say, that love is a thing brought out by nature. But, I ask, how is it that we who have got the law of God for our guide in addition to our natural advantages, thus tolerate the disturbances and disorders raised by our enemies, who seem inflamed, as it were, with firebrands? How is it, that having eyes, we see not, neither understand, though we are surrounded by the intelligence of the law? What a stupor has seized upon our life, that we are thus neglectful of ourselves, and that although God admonishes us! Is it not an intolerable evil? and ought we not to esteem such men as our enemies, and not the household and people of God? For they are infuriated against us, abandoned as they are: they lay grievous crimes to our charge, and make attacks upon us as enemies.

62. And I would have you yourselves to consider with what exceeding madness they do this. The foolish men carry their maliciousness at their tongues' end. They carry about with them a sort of leaden anger, so that they reciprocally smite one

another, and involve us by way of increasing their own punishment. The good teacher is accounted an enemy, while he who clothes himself with the vice of envy, contrary to all justice makes his gain of the gentle temper of the people; he ravages, and consumes, he decks himself out, and recommends himself with false praises; he subverts the truth, and corrupts the faith, until he finds out a hole and hiding-place for his conscience. Thus their very perverseness makes them wretched, while they impudently prefer themselves to places of honour, however unworthy they may be. Ah! what a mischief is this! they say "Such an one is too old; such an one is a mere boy; the office belongs to me; it is due to me, since it is taken away from him. I will gain over all men to my side, and then I will endeavour with my power to ruin him." Plain indeed is this proclamation of their madness to all the world; the sight of companies, and gatherings, and rowers under command in their offensive cabals. Alas! what preposterous conduct is ours, if I may say it! Do they make an exhibition of their folly in the Church of God? And are they not yet ashamed of themselves? Do they not yet blame themselves? Are they not smitten in their consciences, so that they now at length shew that they entertain a proper sense of their deceit and contentiousness? Theirs is the mere force of envy, supported by those baneful influences which naturally belong to it. But those wretches have no power against your Bishop. Believe me, brethren, their endeavours will have no other effect than this, after they have worn down our days, to leave to themselves no place of repentance in this life. Wherefore I beseech you, lend help to yourselves; receive kindly our love, and with all your strength drive away those who desire to obliterate from among us the grace of unanimity; and looking unto God, love one another. I received gladly your Bishop Athanasius, and addressed him in such a manner, as being persuaded that he was a man of God. It is for you to understand these things, not for me to judge of them. I thought it becoming that the most reverend Athanasius himself should convey my salutation to you, knowing his kind care of you, which, in a manner worthy of that peaceable faith which I myself profess, is continually engaged in the good work of declaring saving knowledge, and will be able to exhort you as is suitable, May God preserve you, beloved brethren.

Such was the letter of Constantine.

63. After these occurrences the Meletians remained quiet for a little time, but afterwards shewed their hostility again, and contrived the following plot, with the aim of pleasing those who had hired their services. The Mareotis is a country district of Alexandria, in which Meletius was not able to make a schism. Now while the Churches still existed within their appointed limits, and all the Presbyters had congregations in them, and while the people were living in peace, a certain person named

Ischyras, who was not a clergyman, but of a worthless disposition, endeavoured to lead astray the people of his own village, declaring himself to be a clergyman. Upon learning this, the Presbyter of the place informed me of it when I was going through my visitation of the Churches, and I sent Macarius the Presbyter with him to summon Ischyras. They found him sick and lying in a cell, and charged his father to admonish his son not to continue any such practices as had been reported against him. But when he recovered from his sickness, being prevented by his friends and his father from pursuing the same course, he fled over to the Meletians; and they communicate with Eusebius and his fellows, and at last that calumny is invented by them, that Macarius had broken a cup, and that a certain Bishop named Arsenius had been murdered by me. Arsenius they placed in concealment, in order that he might seem made away with, when he did not make his appearance; and they carried about a hand, pretending that he had been cut to pieces. As for Ischyras, whom they did not even know, they began to spread a report that he was a Presbyter, in order that what he said about the cup might mislead the people. Ischyras, however, being censured by his friends, came to me weeping, and said that no such thing as they had reported had been done by Macarius, and that himself had been suborned by the Meletians to invent this calumny. And he wrote the following letter.

To the Blessed pope Athanasius, Ischyras sends health in the Lord.

64. As when I came to you, my Lord Bishop, desiring to be received into the Church, you reproved me for what I formerly said, as though I had proceeded to such lengths of my own free choice, I therefore submit to you this my apology in writing, in order that you may understand, that violence was used towards me, and blows inflicted on me by Isaac and Heraclides, and Isaac of Letopolis, and those of their party. And I declare, and take God as my witness in this matter, that of none of the things which they have stated, do I know you to be guilty. For no breaking of a cup or overturning of the Holy Table ever took place, but they compelled me by violent usage to assert all this. And this defence I make and submit to you in writing, desiring and claiming for myself to be admitted among the members of your congregation. I pray that you may have health in the Lord.

I submit this my handwriting to you the Bishop Athanasius in the presence of the Presbyters, Ammonas of Dicella, Heraclius of Phascos, Boccon of Chenebri, Achillas of Myrsine, Didymus of Taphosiris, and Justus from Bomotheus; and of the Deacons, Paul, Peter, and Olympius, of Alexandria, and Ammonius, Pistus, Demetrius, and Gaius, of the Mareotis.

65. Notwithstanding this statement of Ischyras, they again spread abroad the same charges against me everywhere, and also reported them to the Emperor Constantine. He too had heard before of the affair of the cup in Psammathia, when I was there, and had detected the falsehood of my enemies. But now he wrote to Antioch to Dalmatius the Censor requiring him to institute a judicial enquiry respecting the murder. Accordingly the Censor sent me notice to prepare for my defence against the charge. Upon receiving his letters, although at first I paid no regard to the thing because I knew that nothing of what they said was true, yet seeing that the Emperor was moved, I wrote to my fellow-ministers into Egypt, and sent a deacon, desiring to learn something of Arsenius, for I had not seen the man for five or six years. Well, not to relate the matter at length, Arsenius was found in concealment, in the first instance in Egypt, and afterwards my friends discovered him again in concealment in Tyre also. And what was most remarkable, even when he was discovered he would not confess that he was Arsenius, until he was convicted in court before Paul, who was then Bishop of Tyre, and at last out of very shame could not deny it.

This he did in order to fulfil his contract with Eusebius and his fellows, lest, if he were discovered, the game they were playing should at length be broken up; which in fact came to pass. For when I wrote the Emperor word, that Arsenius was discovered, and reminded him of what he had heard in Psammathia concerning Macarius the Presbyter, he stopped the proceedings of the Censor's court, and wrote condemning the proceedings against me as calumnious, and commanded Eusebius and his fellows, who were coming into the East to appear against me, to return. Now in order to shew that they accused me of having murdered Arsenius (not to bring forward the letters of many persons on the subject), it shall be sufficient only to produce one from Alexander the Bishop of Thessalonica, from which the tenor of the rest may be inferred. He then being acquainted with the reports which Archaph, who is also called John, circulated against me on the subject of the murder, and having heard that Arsenius was alive, wrote as follows.

Letter of Alexander.

To his dearly beloved son and fellow-minister like-minded, the lord Athanasius, Alexander the Bishop sends health in the Lord.

66. I congratulate the most excellent Sarapion, that he is striving so earnestly to adorn himself with holy habits, and is thus advancing to higher praise the memory of his father. For, as the Holy Scripture somewhere says, though his father die, yet he is as though he were not dead:' for he has left behind him a memorial of his life. What my feelings were towards the ever memorable Sozon, you yourself, my

lord, are not ignorant, for you know the sacredness of his memory, as well as the goodness of the young man. I have received only one letter from your reverence, which I had by the hands of this youth. I mention this to you, my lord, in order that you may know. Our dearly beloved brother and deacon Macarius, afforded me great pleasure by writing to me from Constantinople, that the false accuser Archaph had met with disgrace, for having given out before all men that a live man had been murdered. That he will receive from the righteous Judge, together with all the tribe of his associates, that punishment, which his crimes deserve, the unerring Scriptures assure us. May the Lord of all preserve you for very many years, my lord, in every way most kind.

67. And they who lived with Arsenius bear witness, that he was kept in concealment for this purpose, that they might pretend his death; for in searching after him we found the person [who had done so], and he in consequence wrote the following letter to John, who played the chief part in this false accusation.

To his dearly beloved brother John, Pinnes, Presbyter of the Monastery of Ptemencyrcis, in the home of Anteopolis, sends greeting.

I wish you to know, that Athanasius sent his deacon into the Thebais, to search everywhere for Arsenius;

and Pecysius the Presbyter, and Silvanus the brother of Helias, and Tapenacerameus, and Paul monk of Hypsele, whom he first fell in with, confessed that Arsenius was with us. Upon learning this we caused him to be put on board a vessel, and to sail to the lower countries with Helias the monk. Afterwards the deacon returned again suddenly with certain others, and entered our monastery, in search of the same Arsenius, and him they found not, because, as I said before, we had sent him away to the lower countries; but they conveyed me together with Helias the monk, who took him out of the way, to Alexandria, and brought us before the Duke; when I was unable to deny, but confessed that he was alive, and had not been murdered: the monk also who took him out of the way confessed the same. Wherefore I acquaint you with these things, Father, lest you should determine to accuse Athanasius; for I said that he was alive, and had been concealed with us, and all this is become known in Egypt, and it cannot any longer be kept secret.

I, Paphnutius, monk of the same monastery, who wrote this letter, heartily salute you. I pray for your health.

The following also is the letter which the Emperor wrote when he learnt that Arsenius was found to be alive. Constantine, Victor, Maximus, Augustus, to the pope Athanasius.

68. Having read the letters of your wisdom, I felt the inclination to write in return to your fortitude, and to exhort you that you would endeavour to restore the people of God to tranquillity, and to merciful feelings. For in my own mind I hold these things to be of the greatest importance, that we should cultivate truth, and ever keep righteousness in our thoughts, and have pleasure especially in those who walk in the right way of life. But as concerning those who are deserving of all execration, I mean the most perverse and ungodly Meletians, who have at last stultified themselves by their folly, and are now raising unreasonable commotions by envy, uproar, and tumult, thus making manifest their own ungodly dispositions, I will say thus much. You see that those who they pretended had been slain with the sword, are still amongst us, and in the enjoyment of life. Now what could be a stronger presumption against them, and one so manifestly and clearly tending to their condemnation, as that those whom they declared to have been murdered, are yet in the enjoyment of life, and accordingly will be able to speak for themselves?

But this further accusation was advanced by these same Meletians. They positively affirmed that you, rushing in with lawless violence, had seized upon and broken a cup, which was deposited in the most Holy Place; than which there certainly could not be a more serious charge, nor a more grievous offence, had such a crime actually been perpetrated. But what manner of accusation is this? What is the meaning of this change and variation and difference in the circumstances of it, insomuch that they now transfer this same accusation to another person, a fact which makes it clearer, so to speak, than the light itself, that they designed to lay a plot for your wisdom? After this, who can be willing to follow them, men that have fabricated such charges to the injury of another, seeing too that they are hurrying themselves on to ruin, and are conscious that they are accusing you of false and feigned crimes? Who then, as I said, will follow after them, and thus go headlong in the way of destruction; in that way in which it seems they alone suppose that they have hope of safety and of help? But if they were willing to walk according to a pure conscience, and to be directed by the best wisdom, and to go in the way of a sound mind, they would easily perceive that no help can come to them from Divine Providence, while they are given up to such doings, and tempt their own destruction. I should not call this a harsh judgment of them, but the simple truth.

And finally, I will add, that I wish this letter to be read frequently by your wisdom in public, that it may thereby come to the knowledge of all men, and especially reach the ears of those who thus act, and thus raise disturbances; for the judgment which is expressed by me according to the dictates of equity is confirmed also by real facts. Wherefore, seeing that in such conduct there is so great an offence, let them understand that I have thus judged; and that I have come to this determination, that if they excite any further commotion of this kind, I will myself in person take cognizance of the matter, and that not according to the ecclesiastical, but according to the civil laws, and so I will in future find them out, because they clearly are robbers, so to speak, not only against human kind, but against the divine doctrine itself. May God ever preserve you, beloved brother!

69. But that the wickedness of the calumniators might be more fully displayed, behold Arsenius also wrote to me after he was discovered in his place of concealment; and as the letter which Ischyras had written confessed the falsehood of their accusation, so that of Arsenius proved their maliciousness still more completely.

To the blessed Pope Athanasius, Arsenius, Bishop of those who were heretofore under Meletius in the city of the Hypselites, together with the Presbyters and Deacons, wishes much health in the Lord. Being earnestly desirous of peace and union with the Catholic Church, over which by the grace of God you preside, and wishing to submit ourselves to the Canon of the Church, according to the ancient rule, we write unto you, dearly beloved Pope, and declare in the name of the Lord, that we will not for the future hold communion with those who continue in schism, and are not yet at peace with the Catholic Church, whether Bishops, Presbyters, or Deacons.

Neither will we take part with them if they wish to establish anything in a Council; neither will we send letters of peace [687] unto them nor receive such from them; neither yet without the consent of you, the bishop of the metropolis, will we publish any determination concerning Bishops, or on any other general ecclesiastical question; but we will yield obedience to all the canons that have heretofore been ordained, after the example of the Bishops Ammonian, Tyrannus, Plusian, and the rest. Wherefore we beseech your goodness to write to us speedily in answer, and likewise to our fellow-ministers concerning us, informing them that we will henceforth abide by the fore-mentioned resolution and will be at peace with the Catholic Church, and at unity with our fellow-ministers in the [various] districts. And we are persuaded that your prayers, being acceptable unto God, will so prevail with Him, that this peace shall be firm and indissoluble unto the end, according to the will of God the Lord of all, through Jesus Christ our Lord.

The sacred Ministry that is under you, we and those that are with us salute. Very shortly, if God permit, we will come to visit your goodness. I, Arsenius, pray for your health in the Lord for many years, most blessed Pope.

70. But a stronger and clearer proof of the calumny against us is the recantation of John, of which the most God-beloved Emperor Constantine of blessed

memory is a witness, for knowing how John had accused himself, and having received letters from him expressing his repentance, he wrote to him as follows.

Constantine, Maximus, Augustus to John. The letters which I have received from your prudence were extremely pleasing to me, because I learned from them what I very much longed to hear, that you had laid aside every petty feeling, had joined the Communion of the Church as became you, and were now in perfect concord with the most reverend Bishop Athanasius. Be assured therefore that so far I entirely approve of your conduct; because, giving up all skirmishing, you have done that which is pleasing to God, and have embraced the unity of His Church. In order therefore that you may obtain the accomplishment of your wishes, I have thought it right to grant you permission to enter the public conveyance, and to come to the court of my clemency. Let it then be your care to make no delay; but as this letter gives you authority to use the public conveyance, come to me immediately, that you may have your desires fulfilled, and by appearing in my presence may enjoy that pleasure which it is fit for you to receive. May God preserve you continually, dearly beloved brother.

Chapter 6

Documents connected with the Council of Tyre.

71. Thus ended the conspiracy. The Meletians were repulsed and covered with shame; but notwithstanding this Eusebius and his fellows still did not remain quiet, for it was not for the Meletians but for Arius and his fellows, that they cared, and they were afraid lest, if the proceedings of the former should be stopped, they should no longer find persons to play the parts, by whose assistance they might bring in that heresy. They therefore again stirred up the Meletians, and persuaded the Emperor to give orders that a Council should be held afresh at Tyre, and Count Dionysius was despatched thither, and a military guard was given to Eusebius and his fellows. Macarius also was sent as a prisoner to Tyre under a guard of soldiers; and the Emperor wrote to me, and laid a peremptory command upon me, so that, however unwilling, I set out. The whole conspiracy may be understood from the letters which the Bishops of Egypt wrote; but it will be necessary to relate how it was contrived by them in the outset, that so may be perceived the malice and wickedness that was exercised against me. There are in Egypt, Libya, and Pentapolis, nearly one hundred Bishops; none of whom laid anything to my charge; none of the Presbyters found any fault with me; none of the people spoke aught against me; but it was the Meletians who were ejected by Peter, and the Arians,

that divided the plot between them, while the one party claimed to themselves the right of accusing me, the other of sitting in judgment on the case. I objected to Eusebius and his fellows as being my enemies on account of the heresy; next, I shewed in the following manner that the person who was called my accuser was not a Presbyter at all. When Meletius was admitted into communion (would that he had never been so admitted!) the blessed Alexander who knew his craftiness required of him a schedule of the Bishops whom he said he had in Egypt, and of the presbyters and deacons that were in Alexandria itself, and if he had any in the country district. This the Pope Alexander has done, lest Meletius, having received the freedom of the Church, should tender [693] many, and thus continually, by a fraudulent procedure, foist upon us whomsoever he pleased. Accordingly he has made out the following schedule of those in Egypt.

A schedule presented by Meletius to the Bishop Alexander.

I, Meletius of Lycopolis, Lucius of Antinopolis, Phasileus of Hermopolis, Achilles of Cusae, Ammonius of Diospolis.

In Ptolemais, Pachymes of Tentyrae.

In Maximianopolis, Theodorus of Coptus.

In Thebais, Cales of Hermethes, Colluthus of Upper Cynopolis, Pelagius of Oxyrynchus, Peter of Heracleopolis, Theon of Nilopolis, Isaac of Letopolis, Heraclides of Niciopolis, Isaac of Cleopatris, Melas of Arsenoitis.

In Heliopolis, Amos of Leontopolis, Ision of Athribis.

In Pharbethus, Harpocration of Bubastus, Moses of Phacusae, Callinicus of Pelusium, Eudaemon of Tanis, Ephraim of Thmuis.

In Sais, Hermaeon of Cynopolis and Busiris, Soterichus of Sebennytus, Pininuthes of Phthenegys, Cronius of Metelis, Agathammon of the district of Alexandria.

In Memphis, John who was ordered by the Emperor to be with the Archbishop. These are those of Egypt.

And the Clergy that he had in Alexandria were Apollonius Presbyter, Irenaeus Presbyter, Dioscorus Presbyter, Tyrannus Presbyter. And Deacons; Timotheus Deacon, Antinous Deacon, Hephaestion Deacon. And Macarius Presbyter of Parembole.

72. These Meletius presented actually in person to the Bishop Alexander, but he made no mention of the person called Ischyras, nor ever professed at all that he had any Clergy in the Mareotis.

Notwithstanding our enemies did not desist from their attempts, but still he that was no Presbyter was feigned to be one, for there was the Count ready to use compulsion towards us, and soldiers were hurrying us about. But even then the grace of God prevailed: for they could not convict Macarius in the matter of the cup; and Arsenius, whom they reported to have been murdered by me, stood before them alive and shewed the falseness of their accusation. When therefore they were unable to convict Macarius, Eusebius and his fellows, who became enraged that they had lost the prey of which they had been in pursuit, persuaded the Count Dionysius, who is one of them, to send to the Mareotis, in order to see whether they could not find out something there against the Presbyter, or rather that they might at a distance patch up their plot as they pleased in our absence: for this was their aim. However,—when we represented that the journey to the Mareotis was a superfluous undertaking (for that they ought not to pretend that statements were defective which they had been employed upon so long, and ought not now to defer the matter; for they had said whatever they thought they could say, and now being at a loss what to do, they were making pretences); or if they must needs go to the Mareotis, that at least the suspected parties should not be sent,—the Count was convinced by my reasoning, with respect to the suspected persons; but they did anything rather than what I proposed, for the very persons whom I objected against on account of the Arian heresy, these were they who promptly went off, viz. Diognius, Maris, Theodorus, Macedonius, Ursacius, and Valens. Again, letters were written to the Prefect of Egypt and a military guard was provided; and, what was remarkable and altogether most suspicious, they caused Macarius the accused party to remain behind under a guard of soldiers, while they took with them the accuser. Now who after this does not see through this conspiracy? Who does not clearly perceive the wickedness of Eusebius and his fellows? For if a judicial enquiry must needs take place in the Mareotis, the accused also ought to have been sent thither. But if they did not go for the purpose of such an enquiry, why did they take the accuser? It was enough that he had not been able to prove the fact. But this they did in order that they might carry on their designs against the absent Presbyter, whom they could not convict when present, and might concoct a plan as they pleased. For when the Presbyters of Alexandria and of the whole district found fault with them because they were there by themselves, and required that they too might be present at their proceedings (for they said that they knew both the circumstances of the case, and the history of the person named Ischyras), they would not allow them; and although they had with them Philagrius the Prefect of Egypt, who was an apostate, and heathen soldiers, during an enquiry which it was not becoming even for Catechumens to witness, they would not admit the Clergy, lest there as well as at Tyre there might be those who would expose them.

73. But in spite of these precautions they were not able to escape detection: for the Presbyters of the City and of the Mareotis, perceiving their evil designs, addressed to them the following protest.

To Theognius, Maris, Macedonius, Theodorus, Ursacius, and Valens, the Bishops who have come from Tyre, these from the Presbyters and Deacons of the Catholic Church of Alexandria under the most reverend Bishop Athanasius.

It was incumbent upon you when you came hither and brought with you the accuser, to bring also the Presbyter Macarius; for trials are appointed by Holy Scripture to be so constituted, that the accuser and accused may stand up together. But since neither you brought Macarius, nor our most reverend Bishop Athanasius came hither with you, we claimed for ourselves the right of being present at the investigation, that we might see that the enquiry was conducted impartially, and might ourselves be convinced of the truth. But when you refused to allow this, and wished, in company only with the Prefect of Egypt and the accuser, to do whatever you pleased, we confess that we saw a suspicion of evil in the affair, and perceived that your coming was only the act of a cabal and a conspiracy. Wherefore we address to you this letter, to be a testimony before a genuine Council, that it may be known to all men, that you have carried on an ex parte proceeding and for your own ends, and have desired nothing else but to form a conspiracy against us. A copy of this, lest it should be kept secret by you, we have handed in to Palladius also the Controller of Augustus. For what you have already done causes us to suspect you, and to reckon on the like conduct from you hereafter.

I Dionysius Presbyter have handed in this letter. Alexander Presbyter, Nilaras Presbyter, Longus Presbyter, Aphthonius Presbyter, Athanasius Presbyter, Amyntius Presbyter, Pistus Presbyter, Plution Presbyter, Dioscorus Presbyter, Apollonius Presbyter, Sarapion Presbyter, Ammonius Presbyter, Gaius Presbyter, Rhinus Presbyter, AEthales Presbyter.

Deacons; Marcellinus Deacon, Appianus Deacon, Theon Deacon, Timotheus Deacon, a second Timotheus Deacon.

74. This is the letter, and these the names of the Clergy of the city; and the following was written by the Clergy of the Mareotis, who know the character of the accuser, and who were with me in my visitation.

To the holy Council of blessed Bishops of the Catholic Church, all the Presbyters and Deacons of the Mareotis send health in the Lord.

Knowing that which is written, Speak that thine eyes have seen,' and, A false witness shall not be unpunished', we testify what we have seen, especially since the conspiracy which has been formed against our Bishop Athanasius has made our testimony necessary. We wonder how Ischyras ever came to be reckoned among the number of the Ministers of the Church, which is the first point we think it necessary to mention. Ischyras never was a Minister of the Church; but when formerly he represented himself to be a Presbyter of Colluthus, he found no one to believe him, except only his own relations. For he never had a Church, nor was ever considered a Clergyman by those who lived but a short distance from his village, except only, as we said before, by his own relations. But, notwithstanding he assumed this designation, he was deposed in the presence of our Father Hosius at the Council which assembled at Alexandria, and was admitted to communion as a layman, and so he continued subsequently, having fallen from his falsely reputed rank of presbyter. Of his character we think it unnecessary to speak, as all men have it in their power to become acquainted therewith. But since he has falsely accused our Bishop Athanasius of breaking a cup and overturning a table, we are necessarily obliged to address you on this point. We have said already that he never had a Church in the Mareotis; and we declare before God as our witness, that no cup was broken, nor table overturned by our Bishop, nor by any one of those who accompanied him; but all that is alleged respecting this affair is mere calumny. And this we say, not as having been absent from the Bishop, for we are all with him when he makes his visitation of the Mareotis, and he never goes about alone, but is accompanied by all of us Presbyters and Deacons, and by a considerable number of the people. Wherefore we make these assertions as having been present with him in every visitation which he has made amongst us, and testify that neither was a cup ever broken, nor table overturned, but the whole story is false, as the accuser himself also witnesses under his own hand. For when, after he had gone off with Meletians, and had reported these things against our Bishop Athanasius, he wished to be admitted to communion, he was not received, although he wrote and confessed under his own hand that none of these things were true, but that he had been suborned by certain persons to say so.

75. Wherefore also Theognius, Theodorus, Maris, Macedonius, Ursacius, Valens, and their fellows came into the Mareotis, and when they found that none of these things were true, but it was likely to be discovered that they had framed a false accusation against our Bishop Athanasius, Theognius and his fellows being themselves his enemies, caused the relations of Ischyras and certain Arian madmen to say whatever they wished. For none of the people spoke against the Bishop; but these persons, through fear of Philagrius the Prefect of Egypt, and by threats and with the support of the Arian madmen, accomplished whatever they desired. For when we came to disprove the calumny, they would not

permit us, but cast us out, while they admitted whom they pleased to a participation in their schemes, and concerted matters with them, influencing them by fear of the Prefect Philagrius. Through his means they prevented us from being present, that we might discover whether those who were suborned by them were members of the Church or Arian madmen. And you also, dearly beloved Fathers, know, as you teach us, that the testimony of enemies avails nothing. That what we say is the truth the handwriting of Ischyras testifies, as do also the facts themselves, because when we were conscious that no such thing as was pretended had taken place, they took with them Philagrius, that through fear of the sword and by threats they might frame whatever plots they wished. These things we testify as in the presence of God; we make these assertions as knowing that there will be a judgment held by God; desiring indeed all of us to come to you, but being content with certain of our number, so that the letters may be instead of the presence of those who have not come.

I, Ingenius Presbyter, pray you health in the Lord, beloved fathers. Theon Presbyter, Ammonas P., Heraclius P., Boccon P., Tryphon P., Peter P., Hierax P., Sarapion P., Marcus P., Ptollarion P., Gaius P., Dioscorus P., Demetrius P., Thyrsus P.

Deacons; Pistus Deacon, Apollos D., Serras D., Pistus D., Polynicus D., Ammonius D., Maurus D.,

Hephaestus D., Apollos D., Metopas D., Apollos D., Serapas D., Meliphthongus D., Lucius D., Gregoras D.

76. The same to the Controller, and to Philagrius, at that time Prefect of Egypt.

To Flavius Philagrius, and to Flavius Palladius, Ducenary, Officer of the Palace, and Controller, and to Flavius Antoninus, Commissary of Provisions, and Centenary of my lords the most illustrious Prefects of the sacred Praetorium, these from the Presbyters and Deacons of the Mareotis, a nome of the Catholic Church which is under the most Reverend Bishop Athanasius, we address this testimony by those whose names are underwritten:–

Whereas Theognius, Maris, Macedonius, Theodorus, Ursacius, and Valens, as if sent by all the Bishops who assembled at Tyre, came into our Diocese alleging that they had received orders to investigate certain ecclesiastical affairs, among which they spoke of the breaking of a cup of the Lord, of which information was given them by Ischyras, whom they brought with them, and who says that he is a Presbyter, although he is not,–for he was ordained by the Presbyter Colluthus who pretended to the Episcopate, and was afterwards ordered by a whole Council, by Hosius and the Bishops that were with him, to take the place of a Presbyter, as he was before; and accordingly all that were ordained by

Colluthus resumed the same rank which they held before, and so Ischyras himself proved to be a layman,–and the church which he says he has, never was a church at all, but a quite small private house belonging to an orphan boy of the name of Ision;– for this reason we have offered this testimony, adjuring you by Almighty God, and by our Lords Constantine Augustus, and the most illustrious Caesars his sons, to bring these things to the knowledge of their piety. For neither is he a Presbyter of the Catholic Church nor does he possess a church, nor has a cup ever been broken, but the whole story is false and an invention.

Dated in the Consulship of Julius Constantius the most illustrious Patrician, brother of the most religious Emperor Constantine Augustus, and of Rufinus Albinus, most illustrious men, on the tenth day of the month Thoth.

These were the letters of the Presbyters.

77. The following also are the letters and protests of the Bishops who came with us to Tyre, when they became aware of the conspiracy and plot.

To the Bishops assembled at Tyre, most honoured Lords, those of the Catholic Church who have come from Egypt with Athanasius send greeting in the Lord.

We suppose that the conspiracy which has been formed against us by Eusebius, Theognius, Maris, Narcissus, Theodorus, Patrophilus, and their fellows is no longer uncertain. From the very beginning we all demurred, through our fellow-minister Athanasius, to the holding of the enquiry in their presence, knowing that the presence of even one enemy only, much more of many, is able to disturb and injure the hearing of a cause. And you also yourselves know the enmity which they entertain, not only towards us, but towards all the orthodox, how that for the sake of the madness of Arius, and his impious doctrine, they direct their assaults, they form conspiracies against all. And when, being confident in the truth, we desired to shew the falsehood, which the Meletians had employed against the Church, Eusebius and his fellows endeavoured by some means or other to interrupt our representations, and strove eagerly to set aside our testimony, threatening those who gave an honest judgment, and insulting others, for the sole purpose of carrying out the design they had against us. Your godly piety, most honoured Lords, was probably ignorant of their conspiracy, but we suppose that it has now been made manifest. For indeed they have themselves plainly disclosed it; for they desired to send to the Mareotis those of their party who are suspected by us, so that, while we were absent and remained here, they might disturb the people and accomplish what they wished. They knew that the Arian madmen, and Colluthians and Meletians, were enemies of the Catholic Church and therefore they were anxious to send them, that in the presence of our enemies they might devise against us whatever schemes they pleased. And those of the Meletians who are here, even four days previously (as they knew that this enquiry was about to take place), despatched at evening certain of their party, as couriers, for the purpose of collecting Meletians out of Egypt into the Mareotis, because there were none at all there, and Colluthians and Arian madmen, from other parts, and to prepare them to speak against us. For you also know that Ischyras himself confessed before you, that he had not more than seven persons in his congregation. When therefore we heard that, after they had made what preparations they pleased against us, and had sent these suspected persons, they were going about to each of you, and requiring your subscriptions, in order that it might appear as if this had been done with the consent of you all; for this reason we hastened to write to you, and to present this our testimony; declaring that we are the objects of a conspiracy under which we are suffering by and through them, and demanding that having the fear of God in your minds, and condemning their conduct in sending whom they pleased without our consent, you would refuse your subscriptions, lest they pretend that those things are done by you, which they are contriving only among themselves. Surely it becomes those who are in Christ, not to regard human motives, but to prefer the truth before all things. And be not afraid of their threatenings, which they employ against all, nor of their plots, but rather fear God. If it was at all necessary that persons should be sent to the Mareotis, we also ought to have been there with them, in order that we might convict the enemies of the Church, and point out those who were aliens, and that the investigation of the matter might be impartial. For you know that Eusebius and his fellows contrived that a letter should be presented, as coming from the Collutians, the Meletians, and Arians, and directed against us: but it is evident that these enemies of the Catholic Church speak nothing that is true concerning us, but say everything against us. And the law of God forbids an enemy to be either a witness or a judge. Wherefore as you will have to give an account in the day of judgment, receive this testimony, and recognising the conspiracy which has been framed against us, beware, if you are requested by them, of doing anything against us, and of taking part in the designs of Eusebius and his fellows. For you know, as we said before, that they are our enemies, and you are aware why Eusebius of Caesarea became such last year. We pray that you may be in health, greatly beloved Lords.

78. To the most illustrious Count Flavius Dionysius, from the Bishops of the Catholic Church in Egypt who have come to Tyre.

We suppose that the conspiracy which has been formed against us by Eusebius, Theognius, Maris, Narcissus, Theodorus, Patrophilus and their fellows, is no longer uncertain. From the very beginning we all demurred, through our fellow-minister Athanasius, to the holding of the enquiry in their presence, knowing that the presence of even one enemy only, much more of many, is able to disturb and injure the hearing of a cause. For their enmity is manifest which they entertain, not only towards us, but also towards all the orthodox, because they direct their assaults, they form conspiracies against all. And when, being confident in the truth, we desired to shew the falsehood which the Meletians had employed against the Church, Eusebius and his fellows endeavoured by some means or other to interrupt our representations, and strove eagerly to set aside our testimony, threatening those who gave an honest judgment and insulting others, for the sole purpose of carrying out the design they had against us. Your goodness was probably ignorant of the conspiracy which they have formed against us, but we suppose that it has now been made manifest. For indeed they have themselves plainly disclosed it; for they desired to send to the Mareotis those of their party who are suspected by us, so that, while we were absent and remained here, they might disturb the people and accomplish what they wished. They knew that Arian madmen, Colluthians, and Meletians were enemies of the Church, and therefore they were anxious to send them, that in the presence of our enemies, they might devise against us whatever schemes they pleased. And those of the Meletians who are here, even four days previously (as they knew that this enquiry was about to take place), despatched at evening two individuals of their own party, as couriers, for the purpose of collecting Meletians out of Egypt into the Mareotis, because there were none at all there, and Colluthians, and Arian madmen, from other parts, and to prepare them to speak against us. And your goodness knows that he himself confessed before you, that he had not more than seven persons in his congregation. When therefore we heard that, after they had made what preparations they pleased against us, and had sent these suspected persons, they were going about to each of the Bishops and requiring their subscriptions, in order that it might appear that this was done with the consent of them all; for this reason we hastened to refer the matter to your honour, and to present this our testimony, declaring that we are the objects of a conspiracy, under which we are suffering by and through them, and demanding of you that having in your mind the fear of God, and the pious commands of our most religious Emperor, you would no longer tolerate these persons, but condemn their conduct in sending whom they pleased without our consent.

I Adamantius Bishop have subscribed this letter, Ischyras, Ammon, Peter, Ammonianus, Tyrannus, Taurinus, Sarapammon, AElurion, Harpocration,

Moses, Optatus, Anubion, Saprion, Apollonius, Ischyrion, Arbaethion, Potamon, Paphnutius, Heraclides, Theodorus, Agathammon, Gaius, Pistus, Athas, Nicon, Pelagius, Theon, Paninuthius, Nonnus, Ariston, Theodorus, Irenaeus, Blastammon, Philippus, Apollos, Dioscorus, Timotheus of Diospolis, Macarius, Heraclammon, Cronius, Myis, Jacobus, Ariston, Artemidorus, Phinees, Psais, Heraclides.

Another from the same.

79. The Bishops of the Catholic Church who have come from Egypt to Tyre, to the most illustrious Count Flavius Dionysius.

Perceiving that many conspiracies and plots are being formed against us through the machinations of Eusebius, Narcissus, Flacillus, Theognius, Maris, Theodorus, Patrophilus, and their fellows (against whom we wished at first to enter an objection, but were not permitted), we are constrained to have recourse to the present appeal. We observe also that great zeal is exerted in behalf of the Meletians, and that a plot is laid against the Catholic Church in Egypt in our persons. Wherefore we present this letter to you, beseeching you to bear in mind the Almighty Power of God, who defends the kingdom of our most religious and godly Emperor Constantine, and to reserve the hearing of the affairs which concern us for the most religious Emperor himself. For it is but reasonable, since you were commissioned by his Majesty, that you should reserve the matter for him upon our appealing to his piety. We can no longer endure to be the objects of the treacherous designs of the fore-mentioned Eusebius and his fellows, and therefore we demand that the case be reserved for the most religious and God-beloved Emperor, before whom we shall be able to set forth our own and the Church's just claims. And we are convinced that when his piety shall have heard our cause, he will not condemn us. Wherefore we again adjure you by Almighty God, and by our most religious Emperor, who, together with the children of his piety, has thus ever been victorious and prosperous these many years, that you proceed no further, nor suffer yourselves to move at all in the Council in relation to our affairs, but reserve the hearing of them for his piety. We have likewise made the same representations to my Lords the orthodox Bishops.

80. Alexander, Bishop of Thessalonica, on receiving these letters, wrote to the Count Dionysius as follows.

The Bishop Alexander to my master Dionysius.

I see that a conspiracy has evidently been formed against Athanasius; for they have determined, I know not on what grounds, to send all those to whom he has objected, without giving any information to us, although it was agreed that we should consider together who ought to be sent. Take care therefore that nothing be done rashly (for they have come to me in great alarm, saying that the wild beasts have already roused themselves, and are going to rush upon them; for they had heard it reported, that John had sent certain), lest they be beforehand with us, and concoct what schemes they please. For you know that the Colluthians who are enemies of the Church, and the Arians, and Meletians, are all of them leagued together, and are able to work much evil. Consider therefore what is best to be done, lest some mischief arise, and we be subject to censure, as not having judged the matter fairly. Great suspicions are also entertained of these persons, lest, as being devoted to the Meletians, they should go through those Churches whose Bishops are here, and raise an alarm amongst them, and so disorder the whole of Egypt. For they see that this is already taking place to a great extent.

Accordingly the Count Dionysius wrote to Eusebius and his fellows as follows.

81. This is what I have already mentioned to my lords, Flacillus and his fellows, that Athanasius has come forward and complained that those very persons have been sent whom he objected to; and crying out that he has been wronged and deceived. Alexander the lord of my soul has also written to me on the subject; and that you may perceive that what

his Goodness has said is reasonable, I have subjoined his letter to be read by you. Remember also what I wrote to you before: I impressed upon your Goodness, my lords, that the persons who were sent ought to be commissioned by the general vote and decision of all. Take care therefore lest our proceedings fall under censure, and we give just grounds of blame to those who are disposed to find fault with us. For as the accuser's side ought not to suffer any oppression, so neither ought the defendant's. And I think that there is no slight ground of blame against us, when my lord Alexander evidently disapproves of what we have done.

82. While matters were proceeding thus we withdrew from them, as from an assembly of treacherous men, for whatsoever they pleased they did, whereas there is no man in the world but knows that ex parte proceedings cannot stand good. This the divine law determines; for when the blessed Apostle was suffering under a similar conspiracy and was brought to trial, he demanded, saying, The Jews from Asia ought to have been here before thee, and object, if they had aught against me.' On which occasion Festus also, when the Jews wished to lay such a plot against him, as these men have now laid against me, said, It is not the manner of Romans to deliver any man to die, before that he which is accused have the accuser face to face, and have licence to answer for himself concerning the crime laid against him.' But Eusebius and his fellows both

had the boldness to pervert the law, and have proved more unjust even than those wrong-doers. For they did not proceed privately at the first, but when in consequence of our being present they found themselves weak, then they straightway went out, like the Jews, and took counsel together alone, how they might destroy us and bring in their heresy, as those others demanded Barabbas. For this purpose it was, as they have themselves confessed, that they did all these things.

83. Although these circumstances were amply sufficient for our vindication, yet in order that the wickedness of these men and the freedom of the truth might be more fully exhibited, I have not felt averse to repeat them again, in order to shew that they have acted in a manner inconsistently with themselves, and as men scheming in the dark have fallen foul of their own friends, and while they desired to destroy us have like insane persons wounded themselves. For in their investigation of the subject of the Mysteries, they questioned Jews, they examined Catechumens; Where were you,' they said, when Macarius came and overturned the Table?' They answered, We were within;' whereas there could be no oblation if Catechumens were present. Again, although they had written word everywhere, that Macarius came and overthrew everything, while the Presbyter was standing and celebrating the Mysteries, yet when they questioned whomsoever they pleased, and asked them, Where

was Ischyras when Macarius rushed in?' those persons answered that he was lying sick in a cell. Well, then, he that was lying was not standing, nor was he that lay sick in his cell offering the oblation. Besides whereas Ischyras said that certain books had been burnt by Macarius, they who were suborned to give evidence, declared that nothing of the kind had been done, but that Ischyras spoke falsely. And what is most remarkable, although they had again written word everywhere, that those who were able to give evidence had been concealed by us, yet these persons made their appearance, and they questioned them, and were not ashamed when they saw it proved on all sides that they were slanderers, and were acting in this matter clandestinely, and according to their pleasure. For they prompted the witnesses by signs, while the Prefect threatened them, and the soldiers pricked them with their swords; but the Lord revealed the truth, and shewed them to be slanderers. Therefore also they concealed the minutes of their proceedings, which they retained themselves, and charged those who wrote them to put out of sight, and to commit to no one whomsoever. But in this also they were disappointed; for the person who wrote them was Rufus, who is now public executioner in the Augustalian prefecture, and is able to testify to the truth of this; and Eusebius and his fellows sent them to Rome by the hands of their own friends, and Julius the Bishop transmitted them to me. And now they are mad, because we obtained and read what they wished to conceal.

84. As such was the character of their machinations, so they very soon shewed plainly the reasons of their conduct. For when they went away, they took the Arians with them to Jerusalem, and there admitted them to communion, having sent out a letter concerning them, part of which, and the beginning, is as follows.

The holy Council by the grace of God assembled at Jerusalem, to the Church of God which is in Alexandria, and to the Bishops, Presbyters, and Deacons, in all Egypt, the Thebais, Libya, Pentapolis, and throughout the world, sends health in the Lord.

Having come together out of different Provinces to a great meeting which we have held for the consecration of the Martyry of the Saviour, which has been appointed to the service of God the King of all and of His Christ, by the zeal of our most God-beloved Emperor Constantine, the grace of God hath afforded us more abundant rejoicing of heart; which our most God-beloved Emperor himself hath occasioned us by his letters, wherein he hath stirred us up to do that which is right, putting away all envy from the Church of God, and driving far from us all malice, by which the members of God have been heretofore torn asunder, and that we should with simple and peaceable minds receive Arius and his fellows, whom envy, that enemy of all goodness, has caused for a season to be excluded from the Church.

Our most religious Emperor has also in his letter testified to the correctness of their faith, which he has ascertained from themselves, himself receiving the profession of it from them by word of mouth, and has now made manifest to us by subjoining to his own letters the men's orthodox opinion in writing.

85. Every one that hears of these things must see through their treachery. For they made no concealment of what they were doing; unless perhaps they confessed the truth without wishing it. For if I was the hindrance to the admittance of Arius and his fellows into the Church, and if they were received while I was suffering from their plots, what other conclusion can be arrived at, than that these things were done on their account, and that all their proceedings against me, and the story which they fabricated about the breaking of the cup and the murder of Arsenius, were for the sole purpose of introducing impiety into the Church, and of preventing their being condemned as heretics? For this was what the Emperor threatened formerly in his letters to me. And they were not ashamed to write in the manner they did, and to affirm that those persons whom the whole Ecumenical Council anathematized held orthodox sentiments. And as they undertook to say and do anything without scruple, so they were not afraid to meet together in a corner,' in order to overthrow, as far as was in their power, the authority of so great a Council.

Moreover, the price which they paid for false testimony yet more fully manifests their wickedness and impious intentions. The Mareotis, as I have already said, is a country district of Alexandria, in which there has never been either a Bishop or a Chorepiscopus; but the Churches of the whole district are subject to the Bishop of Alexandria, and each Presbyter has under his charge one of the largest villages, which are about ten or more in number. Now the village in which Ischyras lives is a very small one, and possesses so few inhabitants, that there has never been a church built there, but only in the adjoining village. Nevertheless, they determined, contrary to ancient usage, to nominate a Bishop for this place, and not only so, but even to appoint one, who was not so much as a Presbyter. Knowing as they did the unusual nature of such a proceeding, yet being constrained by the promises they had given in return for his false impeachment of me, they submitted even to this, lest that abandoned person, if he were ungratefully treated by them, should disclose the truth, and thereby shew the wickedness of Eusebius and his fellows. Notwithstanding this he has no church, nor a people to obey him, but is scouted by them all, like a dog, although they have even caused the Emperor to write to the Receiver-General (for everything is in their power), commanding that a church should be built for him, that being possessed of that, his statement may appear credible about the cup and the table. They caused him immediately to be nominated a Bishop also, because if he were without a church, and not even a Presbyter, he would appear to be a false accuser, and a fabricator of the whole matter. At any rate he has no people, and even his own relations are not obedient to him, and as the name which he retains is an empty one, so also the following letter is ineffectual, which he keeps, making a display of it as an exposure of the utter wickedness of himself and of Eusebius and his fellows.

The Letter of the Receiver-General.

Flavius Hemerius sends health to the Tax-collector of the Mareotis.

Ischyras the Presbyter having petitioned the piety of our Lords, Augusti and Caesars, that a Church might be built in the district of Irene, belonging to Secontarurus, their divinity has commanded that this should be done as soon as possible. Take care therefore, as soon as you receive the copy of the sacred Edict, which with all due veneration is placed above, and the Reports which have been formed before my devotion, that you quickly make an abstract of them, and transfer them to the Order book, so that the sacred command may be put in execution.

86. While they were thus plotting and scheming, I went up and represented to the Emperor the unjust conduct of Eusebius and his fellows, for he it was

who had commanded the Council to be held, and his Count presided at it. When he heard my report, he was greatly moved, and wrote to them as follows.

Constantine, Victor, Maximus, Augustus, to the Bishops assembled at Tyre.

I know not what the decisions are which you have arrived at in your Council amidst noise and tumult: but somehow the truth seems to have been perverted in consequence of certain confusions and disorders, in that you, through your mutual contentiousness, which you are resolved should prevail, have failed to perceive what is pleasing to God. However, it will rest with Divine Providence to disperse the mischiefs which manifestly are found to arise from this contentious spirit, and to shew plainly to us, whether you, while assembled in that place, have had any regard for the truth, and whether you have made your decisions uninfluenced by either favour or enmity. Wherefore I wish you all to assemble with all speed before my piety in order that you may render in person a true account of your proceedings.

The reason why I have thought good to write thus to you, and why I summon you before me by letter, you will learn from what I am going to say. As I was entering on a late occasion our all-happy home of Constantinople, which bears our name (I chanced at the time to be on horseback), on a sudden the Bishop Athanasius, with certain others whom he had with him, approached me in the middle of the road, so unexpectedly, as to occasion me much amazement. God, who knoweth all things, is my witness, that I should have been unable at first sight even to recognise him, had not some of my attendants, on my naturally inquiring of them, informed me both who it was, and under what injustice he was suffering. I did not however enter into any conversation with him at that time, nor grant him an interview; but when he requested to be heard I was refusing, and all but gave orders for his removal; when with increasing boldness he claimed only this favour, that you should be summoned to appear, that he might have an opportunity of complaining before me in your presence, of the ill-treatment he has met with. As this appeared to me to be a reasonable request, and suitable to the times, I willingly ordered this letter to be written to you, in order that all of you, who constituted the Council which was held at Tyre, might hasten without delay to the Court of my clemency, so as to prove by facts that you had passed an impartial and uncorrupt judgment. This, I say, you must do before me, whom not even you will deny to be a true servant of God.

For indeed through my devotion to God, peace is preserved everywhere, and the Name of God is truly worshipped even by the barbarians, who have hitherto been ignorant of the truth. And it is manifest, that he who is ignorant of the truth, does not know God either. Nevertheless, as I said before, even the barbarians have now come to the knowledge of God, by means of me, His true servant, and have learned to fear Him Whom they perceive from actual facts to be my shield and protector everywhere. And from this chiefly they have come to know God, Whom they fear through the dread which they have of me. But we, who are supposed to set forth (for I will not say to guard) the holy mysteries of His Goodness, we, I say, engage in nothing but what tends to dissension and hatred, and, in short, whatever contributes to the destruction of mankind. But hasten, as I said before, and all of you with all speed come to us, being persuaded that I shall endeavour with all my might to amend what is amiss, so that those things specially may be preserved and firmly established in the law of God, to which no blame nor dishonour may attach; while the enemies of the law, who under pretence of His holy Name bring in manifold and divers blasphemies, shall be scattered abroad, and entirely crushed, and utterly destroyed.

87. When Eusebius and his fellows read this letter, being conscious of what they had done, they prevented the rest of the Bishops from going up, and only themselves went, viz. Eusebius, Theognius, Patrophilus, the other Eusebius, Ursacius, and Valens. And they no longer said anything about the cup and Arsenius (for they had not the boldness to do so), but inventing another accusation which

concerned the Emperor himself, they declared before him, that Athanasius had threatened that he would cause the corn to be withheld which was sent from Alexandria to his own home. The Bishops Adamantius, Anubion, Agathammon, Arbethion, and Peter, were present and heard this. It was proved also by the anger of the Emperor; for although he had written the preceding letter, and had condemned their injustice, as soon as he heard such a charge as this, he was immediately incensed, and instead of granting me a hearing, he sent me away into Gaul. And this again shews their wickedness further; for when the younger Constantine, of blessed memory, sent me back home, remembering what his father had written, he also wrote as follows.

Constantine Caesar, to the people of the Catholic Church of the city of Alexandria.

I suppose that it has not escaped the knowledge of your pious minds, that Athanasius, the interpreter of the adorable Law, was sent away into Gaul for a time, with the intent that, as the savageness of his bloodthirsty and inveterate enemies persecuted him to the hazard of his sacred life, he might thus escape suffering some irremediable calamity, through the perverse dealing of those evil men. In order therefore to escape this, he was snatched out of the jaws of his assailants, and was ordered to pass some time under my government, and so was supplied abundantly with all necessaries in this city, where he lived, although indeed his celebrated virtue, relying entirely on divine assistance, sets at nought the sufferings of adverse fortune. Now seeing that it was the fixed intention of our master Constantine Augustus, my Father, to restore the said Bishop to his own place, and to your most beloved piety, but he was taken away by that fate which is common to all men, and went to his rest before he could accomplish his wish; I have thought proper to fulfil that intention of the Emperor of sacred memory which I have inherited from him. When he comes to present himself before you, you will learn with what reverence he has been treated. Indeed it is not wonderful, whatever I have done on his behalf; for the thoughts of your longing desire for him, and the appearance of so great a man, moved my soul, and urged me thereto. May Divine Providence continually preserve you, beloved brethren.

Dated from Treveri the 15th before the Calends of July.

88. This being the reason why I was sent away into Gaul, who, I ask again, does not plainly perceive the intention of the Emperor, and the murderous spirit of Eusebius and his fellows, and that the Emperor had done this in order to prevent their forming some more desperate scheme? for he listened to them in simplicity. Such were the practices of Eusebius and his fellows, and such their machinations against me. Who that has witnessed them will deny that nothing

has been done in my favour out of partiality, but that that great number of Bishops both individually and collectively wrote as they did in my behalf and condemned the falsehood of my enemies justly, and in accordance with the truth? Who that has observed such proceedings as these will deny that Valens and Ursacius had good reason to condemn themselves, and to write as they did, to accuse themselves when they repented, choosing rather to suffer shame for a short time, than to undergo the punishment of false accusers for ever and ever?

89. Wherefore also my blessed fellow-ministers, acting justly and according to the laws of the Church, while certain affirmed that my case was doubtful, and endeavoured to compel them to annul the sentence which was passed in my favour, have now endured all manner of sufferings, and have chosen rather to be banished than to see the judgment of so many Bishops reversed. Now if those genuine Bishops had withstood by words only those who plotted against me, and wished to undo all that had been done in my behalf; or if they had been ordinary men, and not the Bishops of illustrious cities, and the heads of great Churches, there would have been room to suspect that in this instance they too had acted contentiously and in order to gratify me. But when they not only endeavoured to convince by argument, but also endured banishment, and one of them is Liberius, Bishop of Rome, (for although he did not endure to the end the sufferings

of banishment, yet he remained in his exile for two years, being aware of conspiracy formed against us), and since there is also the great Hosius, together with the Bishops of Italy, and of Gaul, and others from Spain, and from Egypt, and Libya, and all those from Pentapolis (for although for a little while, through fear of the threats of Constantius, he seemed not to resist them yet the great violence and tyrannical power exercised by Constantius, and the many insults and stripes inflicted upon him, proved that it was not because he gave up my cause, but through the weakness of old age, being unable to bear the stripes, that he yielded to them for a season), therefore I say, it is altogether right that all, as being fully convinced, should hate and abominate the injustice and the violence which they have used towards me; especially as it is well known that I have suffered these things on account of nothing else but the Arian impiety.

90. Now if anyone wishes to become acquainted with my case, and the falsehood of Eusebius and his fellows, let him read what has been written in my behalf, and let him hear the witnesses, not one, or two, or three, but that great number of Bishops; and again let him attend to the witnesses of these proceedings, Liberius and Hosius, and their fellows, who when they saw the attempts made against us, chose rather to endure all manner of sufferings than to give up the truth, and the judgment which had been pronounced in our favour. And this they did

with an honourable and righteous intention, for what they suffered proves to what straits the other Bishops were reduced. And they are memorials and records against the Arian heresy, and the wickedness of false accusers, and afford a pattern and model for those who come after, to contend for the truth unto death, and to abominate the Arian heresy which fights against Christ, and is a forerunner of Antichrist, and not to believe those who attempt to speak against me. For the defence put forth, and the sentence given, by so many Bishops of high character, are a trustworthy and sufficient testimony in our behalf.

Printed in Great Britain
by Amazon

55830700R00092